Access Your Online Resources

Don't miss out on the Online Resources included with your purchase!

Your purchase of this product unlocks access to our Online Resources page. Elevate your study experience with our **interactive practice test interface**, along with all of the additional resources that we couldn't include in this book.

Flip to the Online Resources section at the end of this book to find the link and a QR code to get started!

AP® World History: Modern
Prep Book 2025-2026

3 Full Length Practice Tests

AP® World History Secrets
Review with Online
Video Tutorials

2nd Edition

Copyright © 2025 by Mometrix Media LLC

All rights reserved. This product, or parts thereof, may not be reproduced, stored in a retrieval system, or transmitted in any form or by any means—electronic, mechanical, photocopy, recording, scanning, or other—except for brief quotations in critical reviews or articles, without the prior written permission of the publisher.

Written and edited by Matthew Bowling

Printed in the United States of America

This paper meets the requirements of ANSI/NISO Z39.48-1992 (Permanence of Paper).

Mometrix offers volume discount pricing to institutions. For more information or a price quote, please contact our sales department at sales@mometrix.com or 888-248-1219.

AP® and Advanced Placement® are trademarks registered by the College Board, which is not affiliated with, and does not endorse, this product.

Paperback
ISBN 13: 978-1-5167-2779-7
ISBN 10: 1-5167-2779-7

Dear Future Exam Success Story

First of all, **THANK YOU** for purchasing Mometrix study materials!

Second, congratulations! You are one of the few determined test-takers who are committed to doing whatever it takes to excel on your exam. **You have come to the right place.** We developed these study materials with one goal in mind: to deliver you the information you need in a format that's concise and easy to use.

In addition to optimizing your guide for the content of the test, we've outlined our recommended steps for breaking down the preparation process into small, attainable goals so you can make sure you stay on track.

We've also analyzed the entire test-taking process, identifying the most common pitfalls and showing how you can overcome them and be ready for any curveball the test throws you.

Standardized testing is one of the biggest obstacles on your road to success, which only increases the importance of doing well in the high-pressure, high-stakes environment of test day. Your results on this test could have a significant impact on your future, and this guide provides the information and practical advice to help you achieve your full potential on test day.

Your success is our success

We would love to hear from you! If you would like to share the story of your exam success or if you have any questions or comments in regard to our products, please contact us at **800-673-8175** or **support@mometrix.com**.

Thanks again for your business and we wish you continued success!

Sincerely,
The Mometrix Test Preparation Team

Need more help? Check out our flashcards at:
http://MometrixFlashcards.com/AP

Copyright © 2025 by Mometrix Media LLC. All rights reserved.
Printed in the United States of America

Table of Contents

Introduction	1
Secret Key #1 – Plan Big, Study Small	2
Secret Key #2 – Make Your Studying Count	3
Secret Key #3 – Practice the Right Way	4
Secret Key #4 – Pace Yourself	6
Secret Key #5 – Have a Plan for Guessing	7
Test-Taking Strategies	10
World History: Pre-1400	15
Chapter Quiz	31
World History: 1400 to 1914	32
Chapter Quiz	45
World History: 1914 to Present	46
Chapter Quiz	55
World History: Historiography	56
Chapter Quiz	60
AP Practice Test #1	61
Answer Key and Explanations for Test #1	73
AP Practice Test #2	83
Answer Key and Explanations for Test #2	96
AP Practice Test #3	105
Answer Key and Explanations for Test #3	119
How to Overcome Test Anxiety	128
Online Resources	134

Introduction

Thank you for purchasing this resource! You have made the choice to prepare yourself for a test that could have a huge impact on your future, and this guide is designed to help you be fully ready for test day. Obviously, it's important to have a solid understanding of the test material, but you also need to be prepared for the unique environment and stressors of the test, so that you can perform to the best of your abilities.

For this purpose, the first section that appears in this guide is the **Secret Keys**. We've devoted countless hours to meticulously researching what works and what doesn't, and we've boiled down our findings to the five most impactful steps you can take to improve your performance on the test. We start at the beginning with study planning and move through the preparation process, all the way to the testing strategies that will help you get the most out of what you know when you're finally sitting in front of the test.

We recommend that you start preparing for your test as far in advance as possible. However, if you've bought this guide as a last-minute study resource and only have a few days before your test, we recommend that you skip over the first two Secret Keys since they address a long-term study plan.

If you struggle with **test anxiety**, we strongly encourage you to check out our recommendations for how you can overcome it. Test anxiety is a formidable foe, but it can be beaten, and we want to make sure you have the tools you need to defeat it.

Secret Key #1 – Plan Big, Study Small

There's a lot riding on your performance. If you want to ace this test, you're going to need to keep your skills sharp and the material fresh in your mind. You need a plan that lets you review everything you need to know while still fitting in your schedule. We'll break this strategy down into three categories.

Information Organization

Start with the information you already have: the official test outline. From this, you can make a complete list of all the concepts you need to cover before the test. Organize these concepts into groups that can be studied together, and create a list of any related vocabulary you need to learn so you can brush up on any difficult terms. You'll want to keep this vocabulary list handy once you actually start studying since you may need to add to it along the way.

Time Management

Once you have your set of study concepts, decide how to spread them out over the time you have left before the test. Break your study plan into small, clear goals so you have a manageable task for each day and know exactly what you're doing. Then just focus on one small step at a time. When you manage your time this way, you don't need to spend hours at a time studying. Studying a small block of content for a short period each day helps you retain information better and avoid stressing over how much you have left to do. You can relax knowing that you have a plan to cover everything in time. In order for this strategy to be effective though, you have to start studying early and stick to your schedule. Avoid the exhaustion and futility that comes from last-minute cramming!

Study Environment

The environment you study in has a big impact on your learning. Studying in a coffee shop, while probably more enjoyable, is not likely to be as fruitful as studying in a quiet room. It's important to keep distractions to a minimum. You're only planning to study for a short block of time, so make the most of it. Don't pause to check your phone or get up to find a snack. It's also important to **avoid multitasking**. Research has consistently shown that multitasking will make your studying dramatically less effective. Your study area should also be comfortable and well-lit so you don't have the distraction of straining your eyes or sitting on an uncomfortable chair.

The time of day you study is also important. You want to be rested and alert. Don't wait until just before bedtime. Study when you'll be most likely to comprehend and remember. Even better, if you know what time of day your test will be, set that time aside for study. That way your brain will be used to working on that subject at that specific time and you'll have a better chance of recalling information.

Finally, it can be helpful to team up with others who are studying for the same test. Your actual studying should be done in as isolated an environment as possible, but the work of organizing the information and setting up the study plan can be divided up. In between study sessions, you can discuss with your teammates the concepts that you're all studying and quiz each other on the details. Just be sure that your teammates are as serious about the test as you are. If you find that your study time is being replaced with social time, you might need to find a new team.

Secret Key #2 – Make Your Studying Count

You're devoting a lot of time and effort to preparing for this test, so you want to be absolutely certain it will pay off. This means doing more than just reading the content and hoping you can remember it on test day. It's important to make every minute of study count. There are two main areas you can focus on to make your studying count.

Retention

It doesn't matter how much time you study if you can't remember the material. You need to make sure you are retaining the concepts. To check your retention of the information you're learning, try recalling it at later times with minimal prompting. Try carrying around flashcards and glance at one or two from time to time or ask a friend who's also studying for the test to quiz you.

To enhance your retention, look for ways to put the information into practice so that you can apply it rather than simply recalling it. If you're using the information in practical ways, it will be much easier to remember. Similarly, it helps to solidify a concept in your mind if you're not only reading it to yourself but also explaining it to someone else. Ask a friend to let you teach them about a concept you're a little shaky on (or speak aloud to an imaginary audience if necessary). As you try to summarize, define, give examples, and answer your friend's questions, you'll understand the concepts better and they will stay with you longer. Finally, step back for a big picture view and ask yourself how each piece of information fits with the whole subject. When you link the different concepts together and see them working together as a whole, it's easier to remember the individual components.

Finally, practice showing your work on any multi-step problems, even if you're just studying. Writing out each step you take to solve a problem will help solidify the process in your mind, and you'll be more likely to remember it during the test.

Modality

Modality simply refers to the means or method by which you study. Choosing a study modality that fits your own individual learning style is crucial. No two people learn best in exactly the same way, so it's important to know your strengths and use them to your advantage.

For example, if you learn best by visualization, focus on visualizing a concept in your mind and draw an image or a diagram. Try color-coding your notes, illustrating them, or creating symbols that will trigger your mind to recall a learned concept. If you learn best by hearing or discussing information, find a study partner who learns the same way or read aloud to yourself. Think about how to put the information in your own words. Imagine that you are giving a lecture on the topic and record yourself so you can listen to it later.

For any learning style, flashcards can be helpful. Organize the information so you can take advantage of spare moments to review. Underline key words or phrases. Use different colors for different categories. Mnemonic devices (such as creating a short list in which every item starts with the same letter) can also help with retention. Find what works best for you and use it to store the information in your mind most effectively and easily.

Secret Key #3 – Practice the Right Way

Your success on test day depends not only on how many hours you put into preparing, but also on whether you prepared the right way. It's good to check along the way to see if your studying is paying off. One of the most effective ways to do this is by taking practice tests to evaluate your progress. Practice tests are useful because they show exactly where you need to improve. Every time you take a practice test, pay special attention to these three groups of questions:

- The questions you got wrong
- The questions you had to guess on, even if you guessed right
- The questions you found difficult or slow to work through

This will show you exactly what your weak areas are, and where you need to devote more study time. Ask yourself why each of these questions gave you trouble. Was it because you didn't understand the material? Was it because you didn't remember the vocabulary? Do you need more repetitions on this type of question to build speed and confidence? Dig into those questions and figure out how you can strengthen your weak areas as you go back to review the material.

Additionally, many practice tests have a section explaining the answer choices. It can be tempting to read the explanation and think that you now have a good understanding of the concept. However, an explanation likely only covers part of the question's broader context. Even if the explanation makes perfect sense, **go back and investigate** every concept related to the question until you're positive you have a thorough understanding.

As you go along, keep in mind that the practice test is just that: practice. Memorizing these questions and answers will not be very helpful on the actual test because it is unlikely to have any of the same exact questions. If you only know the right answers to the sample questions, you won't be prepared for the real thing. **Study the concepts** until you understand them fully, and then you'll be able to answer any question that shows up on the test.

It's important to wait on the practice tests until you're ready. If you take a test on your first day of study, you may be overwhelmed by the amount of material covered and how much you need to learn. Work up to it gradually.

On test day, you'll need to be prepared for answering questions, managing your time, and using the test-taking strategies you've learned. It's a lot to balance, like a mental marathon that will have a big impact on your future. Like training for a marathon, you'll need to start slowly and work your way up. When test day arrives, you'll be ready.

Start with the strategies you've read in the first two Secret Keys—plan your course and study in the way that works best for you. If you have time, consider using multiple study resources to get different approaches to the same concepts. It can be helpful to see difficult concepts from more than one angle. Then find a good source for practice tests. Many times, the test website will suggest potential study resources or provide sample tests.

Practice Test Strategy

If you're able to find at least three practice tests, we recommend this strategy:

Untimed and Open-Book Practice

Take the first test with no time constraints and with your notes and study guide handy. Take your time and focus on applying the strategies you've learned.

Timed and Open-Book Practice

Take the second practice test open-book as well, but set a timer and practice pacing yourself to finish in time.

Timed and Closed-Book Practice

Take any other practice tests as if it were test day. Set a timer and put away your study materials. Sit at a table or desk in a quiet room, imagine yourself at the testing center, and answer questions as quickly and accurately as possible.

Keep repeating timed and closed-book tests on a regular basis until you run out of practice tests or it's time for the actual test. Your mind will be ready for the schedule and stress of test day, and you'll be able to focus on recalling the material you've learned.

Secret Key #4 – Pace Yourself

Once you're fully prepared for the material on the test, your biggest challenge on test day will be managing your time. Just knowing that the clock is ticking can make you panic even if you have plenty of time left. Work on pacing yourself so you can build confidence against the time constraints of the exam. Pacing is a difficult skill to master, especially in a high-pressure environment, so **practice is vital**.

Set time expectations for your pace based on how much time is available. For example, if a section has 60 questions and the time limit is 30 minutes, you know you have to average 30 seconds or less per question in order to answer them all. Although 30 seconds is the hard limit, set 25 seconds per question as your goal, so you reserve extra time to spend on harder questions. When you budget extra time for the harder questions, you no longer have any reason to stress when those questions take longer to answer.

Don't let this time expectation distract you from working through the test at a calm, steady pace, but keep it in mind so you don't spend too much time on any one question. Recognize that taking extra time on one question you don't understand may keep you from answering two that you do understand later in the test. If your time limit for a question is up and you're still not sure of the answer, mark it and move on, and come back to it later if the time and the test format allow. If the testing format doesn't allow you to return to earlier questions, just make an educated guess; then put it out of your mind and move on.

On the easier questions, be careful not to rush. It may seem wise to hurry through them so you have more time for the challenging ones, but it's not worth missing one if you know the concept and just didn't take the time to read the question fully. Work efficiently but make sure you understand the question and have looked at all of the answer choices, since more than one may seem right at first.

Even if you're paying attention to the time, you may find yourself a little behind at some point. You should speed up to get back on track, but do so wisely. Don't panic; just take a few seconds less on each question until you're caught up. Don't guess without thinking, but do look through the answer choices and eliminate any you know are wrong. If you can get down to two choices, it is often worthwhile to guess from those. Once you've chosen an answer, move on and don't dwell on any that you skipped or had to hurry through. If a question was taking too long, chances are it was one of the harder ones, so you weren't as likely to get it right anyway.

On the other hand, if you find yourself getting ahead of schedule, it may be beneficial to slow down a little. The more quickly you work, the more likely you are to make a careless mistake that will affect your score. You've budgeted time for each question, so don't be afraid to spend that time. Practice an efficient but careful pace to get the most out of the time you have.

Secret Key #5 – Have a Plan for Guessing

When you're taking the test, you may find yourself stuck on a question. Some of the answer choices seem better than others, but you don't see the one answer choice that is obviously correct. What do you do?

The scenario described above is very common, yet most test takers have not effectively prepared for it. Developing and practicing a plan for guessing may be one of the single most effective uses of your time as you get ready for the exam.

In developing your plan for guessing, there are three questions to address:

- When should you start the guessing process?
- How should you narrow down the choices?
- Which answer should you choose?

When to Start the Guessing Process

Unless your plan for guessing is to select C every time (which, despite its merits, is not what we recommend), you need to leave yourself enough time to apply your answer elimination strategies. Since you have a limited amount of time for each question, that means that if you're going to give yourself the best shot at guessing correctly, you have to decide quickly whether or not you will guess.

Of course, the best-case scenario is that you don't have to guess at all, so first, see if you can answer the question based on your knowledge of the subject and basic reasoning skills. Focus on the key words in the question and try to jog your memory of related topics. Give yourself a chance to bring the knowledge to mind, but once you realize that you don't have (or you can't access) the knowledge you need to answer the question, it's time to start the guessing process.

It's almost always better to start the guessing process too early than too late. It only takes a few seconds to remember something and answer the question from knowledge. Carefully eliminating wrong answer choices takes longer. Plus, going through the process of eliminating answer choices can actually help jog your memory.

Summary: Start the guessing process as soon as you decide that you can't answer the question based on your knowledge.

How to Narrow Down the Choices

The next chapter in this book (**Test-Taking Strategies**) includes a wide range of strategies for how to approach questions and how to look for answer choices to eliminate. You will definitely want to read those carefully, practice them, and figure out which ones work best for you. Here though, we're going to address a mindset rather than a particular strategy.

Your odds of guessing an answer correctly depend on how many options you are choosing from.

Number of options left	5	4	3	2	1
Odds of guessing correctly	20%	25%	33%	50%	100%

You can see from this chart just how valuable it is to be able to eliminate incorrect answers and make an educated guess, but there are two things that many test takers do that cause them to miss out on the benefits of guessing:

- Accidentally eliminating the correct answer
- Selecting an answer based on an impression

We'll look at the first one here, and the second one in the next section.

To avoid accidentally eliminating the correct answer, we recommend a thought exercise called **the $5 challenge**. In this challenge, you only eliminate an answer choice from contention if you are willing to bet $5 on it being wrong. Why $5? Five dollars is a small but not insignificant amount of money. It's an amount you could afford to lose but wouldn't want to throw away. And while losing

$5 once might not hurt too much, doing it twenty times will set you back $100. In the same way, each small decision you make—eliminating a choice here, guessing on a question there—won't by itself impact your score very much, but when you put them all together, they can make a big difference. By holding each answer choice elimination decision to a higher standard, you can reduce the risk of accidentally eliminating the correct answer.

The $5 challenge can also be applied in a positive sense: If you are willing to bet $5 that an answer choice *is* correct, go ahead and mark it as correct.

Summary: Only eliminate an answer choice if you are willing to bet $5 that it is wrong.

Which Answer to Choose

You're taking the test. You've run into a hard question and decided you'll have to guess. You've eliminated all the answer choices you're willing to bet $5 on. Now you have to pick an answer. Why do we even need to talk about this? Why can't you just pick whichever one you feel like when the time comes?

The answer to these questions is that if you don't come into the test with a plan, you'll rely on your impression to select an answer choice, and if you do that, you risk falling into a trap. The test writers know that everyone who takes their test will be guessing on some of the questions, so they intentionally write wrong answer choices to seem plausible. You still have to pick an answer though, and if the wrong answer choices are designed to look right, how can you ever be sure that you're not falling for their trap? The best solution we've found to this dilemma is to take the decision out of your hands entirely. Here is the process we recommend:

Once you've eliminated any choices that you are confident (willing to bet $5) are wrong, select the first remaining choice as your answer.

Whether you choose to select the first remaining choice, the second, or the last, the important thing is that you use some preselected standard. Using this approach guarantees that you will not be enticed into selecting an answer choice that looks right, because you are not basing your decision on how the answer choices look.

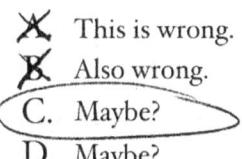

This is not meant to make you question your knowledge. Instead, it is to help you recognize the difference between your knowledge and your impressions. There's a huge difference between thinking an answer is right because of what you know, and thinking an answer is right because it looks or sounds like it should be right.

Summary: To ensure that your selection is appropriately random, make a predetermined selection from among all answer choices you have not eliminated.

Test-Taking Strategies

This section contains a list of test-taking strategies that you may find helpful as you work through the test. By taking what you know and applying logical thought, you can maximize your chances of answering any question correctly!

It is very important to realize that every question is different and every person is different: no single strategy will work on every question, and no single strategy will work for every person. That's why we've included all of them here, so you can try them out and determine which ones work best for different types of questions and which ones work best for you.

Question Strategies

⊘ READ CAREFULLY

Read the question and the answer choices carefully. Don't miss the question because you misread the terms. You have plenty of time to read each question thoroughly and make sure you understand what is being asked. Yet a happy medium must be attained, so don't waste too much time. You must read carefully and efficiently.

⊘ CONTEXTUAL CLUES

Look for contextual clues. If the question includes a word you are not familiar with, look at the immediate context for some indication of what the word might mean. Contextual clues can often give you all the information you need to decipher the meaning of an unfamiliar word. Even if you can't determine the meaning, you may be able to narrow down the possibilities enough to make a solid guess at the answer to the question.

⊘ PREFIXES

If you're having trouble with a word in the question or answer choices, try dissecting it. Take advantage of every clue that the word might include. Prefixes can be a huge help. Usually, they allow you to determine a basic meaning. *Pre-* means before, *post-* means after, *pro-* is positive, *de-* is negative. From prefixes, you can get an idea of the general meaning of the word and try to put it into context.

⊘ HEDGE WORDS

Watch out for critical hedge words, such as *likely, may, can, often, almost, mostly, usually, generally, rarely,* and *sometimes*. Question writers insert these hedge phrases to cover every possibility. Often an answer choice will be wrong simply because it leaves no room for exception. Be on guard for answer choices that have definitive words such as *exactly* and *always*.

⊘ SWITCHBACK WORDS

Stay alert for *switchbacks*. These are the words and phrases frequently used to alert you to shifts in thought. The most common switchback words are *but, although,* and *however*. Others include *nevertheless, on the other hand, even though, while, in spite of, despite,* and *regardless of*. Switchback words are important to catch because they can change the direction of the question or an answer choice.

⊘ Face Value

When in doubt, use common sense. Accept the situation in the problem at face value. Don't read too much into it. These problems will not require you to make wild assumptions. If you have to go beyond creativity and warp time or space in order to have an answer choice fit the question, then you should move on and consider the other answer choices. These are normal problems rooted in reality. The applicable relationship or explanation may not be readily apparent, but it is there for you to figure out. Use your common sense to interpret anything that isn't clear.

Answer Choice Strategies

⊘ Answer Selection

The most thorough way to pick an answer choice is to identify and eliminate wrong answers until only one is left, then confirm it is the correct answer. Sometimes an answer choice may immediately seem right, but be careful. The test writers will usually put more than one reasonable answer choice on each question, so take a second to read all of them and make sure that the other choices are not equally obvious. As long as you have time left, it is better to read every answer choice than to pick the first one that looks right without checking the others.

⊘ Answer Choice Families

An answer choice family consists of two (in rare cases, three) answer choices that are very similar in construction and cannot all be true at the same time. If you see two answer choices that are direct opposites or parallels, one of them is usually the correct answer. For instance, if one answer choice says that quantity x increases and another either says that quantity x decreases (opposite) or says that quantity y increases (parallel), then those answer choices would fall into the same family. An answer choice that doesn't match the construction of the answer choice family is more likely to be incorrect. Most questions will not have answer choice families, but when they do appear, you should be prepared to recognize them.

⊘ Eliminate Answers

Eliminate answer choices as soon as you realize they are wrong, but make sure you consider all possibilities. If you are eliminating answer choices and realize that the last one you are left with is also wrong, don't panic. Start over and consider each choice again. There may be something you missed the first time that you will realize on the second pass.

⊘ Avoid Fact Traps

Don't be distracted by an answer choice that is factually true but doesn't answer the question. You are looking for the choice that answers the question. Stay focused on what the question is asking for so you don't accidentally pick an answer that is true but incorrect. Always go back to the question and make sure the answer choice you've selected actually answers the question and is not merely a true statement.

⊘ Extreme Statements

In general, you should avoid answers that put forth extreme actions as standard practice or proclaim controversial ideas as established fact. An answer choice that states the "process should be used in certain situations, if…" is much more likely to be correct than one that states the "process should be discontinued completely." The first is a calm rational statement and doesn't even make a definitive, uncompromising stance, using a hedge word *if* to provide wiggle room, whereas the second choice is far more extreme.

☑ Benchmark

As you read through the answer choices and you come across one that seems to answer the question well, mentally select that answer choice. This is not your final answer, but it's the one that will help you evaluate the other answer choices. The one that you selected is your benchmark or standard for judging each of the other answer choices. Every other answer choice must be compared to your benchmark. That choice is correct until proven otherwise by another answer choice beating it. If you find a better answer, then that one becomes your new benchmark. Once you've decided that no other choice answers the question as well as your benchmark, you have your final answer.

☑ Predict the Answer

Before you even start looking at the answer choices, it is often best to try to predict the answer. When you come up with the answer on your own, it is easier to avoid distractions and traps because you will know exactly what to look for. The right answer choice is unlikely to be word-for-word what you came up with, but it should be a close match. Even if you are confident that you have the right answer, you should still take the time to read each option before moving on.

General Strategies

☑ Tough Questions

If you are stumped on a problem or it appears too hard or too difficult, don't waste time. Move on! Remember though, if you can quickly check for obviously incorrect answer choices, your chances of guessing correctly are greatly improved. Before you completely give up, at least try to knock out a couple of possible answers. Eliminate what you can and then guess at the remaining answer choices before moving on.

☑ Check Your Work

Since you will probably not know every term listed and the answer to every question, it is important that you get credit for the ones that you do know. Don't miss any questions through careless mistakes. If at all possible, try to take a second to look back over your answer selection and make sure you've selected the correct answer choice and haven't made a costly careless mistake (such as marking an answer choice that you didn't mean to mark). This quick double check should more than pay for itself in caught mistakes for the time it costs.

☑ Pace Yourself

It's easy to be overwhelmed when you're looking at a page full of questions; your mind is confused and full of random thoughts, and the clock is ticking down faster than you would like. Calm down and maintain the pace that you have set for yourself. Especially as you get down to the last few minutes of the test, don't let the small numbers on the clock make you panic. As long as you are on track by monitoring your pace, you are guaranteed to have time for each question.

☑ Don't Rush

It is very easy to make errors when you are in a hurry. Maintaining a fast pace in answering questions is pointless if it makes you miss questions that you would have gotten right otherwise. Test writers like to include distracting information and wrong answers that seem right. Taking a little extra time to avoid careless mistakes can make all the difference in your test score. Find a pace that allows you to be confident in the answers that you select.

⊘ Keep Moving

Panicking will not help you pass the test, so do your best to stay calm and keep moving. Taking deep breaths and going through the answer elimination steps you practiced can help to break through a stress barrier and keep your pace.

Final Notes

The combination of a solid foundation of content knowledge and the confidence that comes from practicing your plan for applying that knowledge is the key to maximizing your performance on test day. As your foundation of content knowledge is built up and strengthened, you'll find that the strategies included in this chapter become more and more effective in helping you quickly sift through the distractions and traps of the test to isolate the correct answer.

Now that you're preparing to move forward into the test content chapters of this book, be sure to keep your goal in mind. As you read, think about how you will be able to apply this information on the test. If you've already seen sample questions for the test and you have an idea of the question format and style, try to come up with questions of your own that you can answer based on what you're reading. This will give you valuable practice applying your knowledge in the same ways you can expect to on test day.

Good luck and good studying!

World History: Pre-1400

Transform passive reading into active learning! After immersing yourself in this chapter, put your comprehension to the test by taking a quiz. The insights you gained will stay with you longer this way. Scan the QR code to go directly to the chapter quiz interface for this study guide. If you're using a computer, simply visit the online resources page at mometrix.com/resources719/apworldhistory-27797 and click the Chapter Quizzes link.

LOWER PALEOLITHIC PERIOD

The **Paleolithic period** is the earliest period of human development, as well as the longest. It is also commonly referred to as the **Old Stone Age**. It lasted from about 2.5 million years ago until about 300,000 years ago. Development during this period was excruciatingly slow. The Paleolithic period is usually divided into three sections: the Lower, Middle, and Upper. The **Lower Paleolithic period** is characterized by the appearance of stone tools; the chopping tools found at the Olduvai Gorge in Tanzania are from this period and date back over a million years. They were probably made by **Australopithecus**, an ancestor of modern humans. Anthropologists have also found stone tools believed to have been made by Homo erectus between 100,000 and 500,000 years ago.

MIDDLE AND UPPER PALEOLITHIC PERIODS

The Middle Paleolithic period occurred about 300,000 years ago until about 40,000 years ago. During this time, the Mousterian culture of Neanderthal men was active in Europe, North Africa, Palestine, and Siberia. These ancestors of modern man lived in caves and had the use of fire. They hunted prehistoric mammals and had slightly more sophisticated tools than their forebears, including crude needles for sewing furs together. These people may have practiced some sort of religion. In the **Upper Paleolithic** period, about 40,000 years ago until about 10,000 years ago, Neanderthals were replaced by varieties of Homo sapiens, including Cro-Magnon man and Grimaldi man. A number of diverse cultures flourished during this period, and the first manmade shelters arose. This was also the period in which people first crafted jewelry and illustrated drawings on the walls of caves.

SOLUTREAN AND MAGDALENIAN PHASE OF THE PALEOLITHIC PERIOD

During the **Upper Paleolithic period**, hunters entered Europe from the east and conquered the more primitive cultures living there. These victorious hunters were known as the **Solutreans**. These people are noted for their fine spearheads, which they used to hunt wild horses. The Solutreans were, in turn, replaced by the **Magdalenians**, the most advanced phase of the Paleolithic period. The Magdalenians subsisted mainly through fishing and reindeer hunting. They developed extremely precise tools and sophisticated weapons, such as the atlatl, a device that made it possible to throw a spear over a great distance. Most of all, though, the Magdalenians are known for their cave paintings in modern-day France.

MESOLITHIC PERIOD

The Mesolithic period, otherwise known as the **Middle Stone Age**, began roughly 10,000 years ago and ended with the introduction of farming (dates vary by culture). In some areas, the use of farming was already beginning at the end of the Paleolithic era, and therefore there may not be a true **Mesolithic period**. The most extensive examples of this kind of culture are found in Northern Europe, where the end of the **Ice Age** created much greater changes in the ability to live off of the land. The remains of the Mesolithic period are mainly just middens (rubbish heaps), as well as some deforestation. The people of the Mesolithic period made small tools out of flint; fishing tackle, canoes, and bows have been found at some sites.

Neolithic Period

The Neolithic period, also known as the **New Stone Age**, refers to that stage of human cultural evolution in which man developed stone tools, settled in villages, and began making crafts. In order to begin living in towns, man had to learn how to domesticate animals and sustain agriculture; formerly, in the Paleolithic and Mesolithic periods, man had subsisted through hunting, fishing, and gathering. The **Neolithic period** is said to have ended when urban civilizations began, or when metal tools or writing began. Because the designation of Neolithic depends on these factors, anthropologists date its occurrence differently for different regions and populations. At present, anthropologists believe that the earliest Neolithic culture was in southwest Asia between 8000 and 6000 BC.

Spread of Neolithic Culture

Most anthropologists date the beginning of **Neolithic culture** at somewhere between 8000 and 6000 BC. It began with the domestication of plants (wheat, barley, and millet) and animals (cattle, sheep, and goats). The Neolithic culture in the valley between the Tigris and Euphrates Rivers gradually evolved into a more urban civilization by 3500 BC. Meanwhile, Neolithic cultural advances spread through Europe, the Nile Valley, the Indus Valley, and the Huang He Valley. In these regions, the innovations of the Neolithic period were intermixed with the particulars of the region; in the Huang He region, for instance, rice cultivation was a product of advances in agriculture. By 1500 BC, Neolithic culture had spread to Mexico and South America. In these areas, corn, beans, and squash were the major crops.

Sumerians of Mesopotamia

Mesopotamia, the region between the Tigris and Euphrates Rivers in what is now considered the Middle East, contained several different early civilizations of which the **Sumerians** were one of the more prominent. They developed the system of writing known as **cuneiform**, by which they elaborated their theories on mathematics and astronomy. The Sumerians also had a detailed system of **laws** and traded widely with other groups throughout the region. They even traded with civilizations as far away as Egypt and India. There was no coin or currency system at this time, thus trade was conducted on the barter system, in which goods are exchanged for one another, directly.

Babylonian Civilization of Mesopotamia

After the Sumerian civilization declined, the next dominant civilization was **Babylon**. The Babylonians conquered the Sumerians and established a city on the Euphrates River in approximately 1,750 B.C. One of the most famous Babylonian rulers was **Hammurabi**, who established the famous **Code of Hammurabi**, an extremely detailed set of laws. This marked the first time that a set of rules governing every aspect of social life was applied to an entire people. The Babylonians are also known for their construction of **ziggurats**, long pyramid-like structures that were used as religious temples. Over time, the Babylonians acquired a reputation as a sensuous and hedonistic people, and the name Babylon has come to stand for any debauched civilization.

> **Review Video: Early Mesopotamia: The Babylonians**
> Visit mometrix.com/academy and enter code: 340325
>
> **Review Video: Early Mesopotamia: The Sumerians**
> Visit mometrix.com/academy and enter code: 939880

PYRAMIDS OF EGYPT

The incredible engineering skills of the Egyptians are most famously displayed in the **pyramids** clustered along the Nile River. These were built roughly between 2700 and 2500 BC. The largest of the structures, the **Khufu pyramid** at Giza, is estimated to have taken 20 years and 100,000 laborers to construct. Today, it stands at 450 feet; some of its height has been lost to erosion. These pyramids were built as burial sites for the pharaohs, who were believed to continue their rule in the afterlife. Peasants worked on the pyramids in exchange for food and shelter. The shape of the pyramids was meant to symbolize the slanting rays of the sun, with sloping sides meant to help the ka (soul) of the pharaoh climb to the sky and join the gods.

> **Review Video: Ancient Egypt**
> Visit mometrix.com/academy and enter code: 398041

RELIGION IN AFRICA

Sub-Saharan Africa was composed of disparate tribes. Most of Africa practiced **animistic religion**, in which it is believed that deities are embodied in the animals that people depend upon for food and service. Ritual and participatory worship were important; common activities included drumming, dancing, divination, and sacrifices. These religions typically had well-developed concepts of good and evil; they believed that some evil, disasters, and illnesses were produced by witchcraft, and that specialists (known as diviners) were required to combat the power of these malevolent beings. Many African peoples shared an underlying belief in a **creator deity**, whose power was expressed through the **ancestors** who founded the tribe. These deceased ancestors were a link between the living and the deities. African tribal religions showed a remarkable resilience when they began to come into contact with monotheistic religions.

INDUS VALLEY CIVILIZATIONS

The **Indus River Valley** is an area bordered by the Himalayan Mountains in what is now Pakistan. The people of this region developed a system of writing, as well as systems of weight and measurement which were useful in trade. They exchanged goods with the people of Mesopotamia in the west, as well as with the people of Tibet in the east. The Aryans invaded this region and brought with them iron technology and the Sanskrit language. The introduction of iron tools made it possible to cultivate the forests of the **Ganges River Valley** in what is now India.

EARLY CITIES OF MOHENJO-DARO AND HARAPPA IN THE INDUS VALLEY

Both the Indus Valley and Egyptian civilizations featured extremely well-planned **cities**. In the Indus Valley, the cities of **Mohenjo-Daro** and **Harappa** were located along the Indus River, in what is now Pakistan. Each of these cities was built around 2500 BC and housed approximately 30,000 citizens. They were each designed in a grid-like pattern, with streets running east-west and north-south. Both Mohenjo-Daro and Harrapa had bathhouses, sewer systems, and organized garbage collection. The structures in these cities were built with oven-fired bricks, which made them durable. Unlike in Egypt, where technological advances were used to enhance religious practice, the people of the Indus Valley used their technology to improve sanitation.

EARLIEST CIVILIZATION IN WHAT WOULD BECOME CHINA

The earliest civilizations in what would become China flourished along the banks of the **Huang He (Yellow) River** before the year 2000 BC. The first Chinese dynasty was the **Xia** (Hsia), succeeded by the **Shang** dynasty. In this period, the rulers established an intricate system of government and a comprehensive judiciary. The basic components of this system would be preserved in Chinese civilization for centuries. The distinctive Chinese style of writing also developed during this period.

Like Egyptian hieroglyphs, the Chinese pictographs were meant to resemble their definition. Over time, though, the Chinese characters have come to resemble their definitions less and less.

ZHOU DYNASTY

The Zhou dynasty, which ran from roughly 1030 to 221 BC, is generally considered to be the third Chinese dynasty, after the Shang. The **Zhou** were brought into power by the commander **Wu**, who declared that the decadent Shang monarchs had forfeited the mandate of heaven (in other words, God's approval of their reign). The Zhou dynasty is generally divided into two parts: The **Western Zhou** ran a feudal-type state in the central plain and the area around the Yellow River. The later **Eastern Zhou** had a more difficult time maintaining control of rival states within its control. The Zhou dynasty was the period in which Chinese civilization spread to most parts of Asia. Both **Confucius** and **Lao Tzu** were active during this period. China became the preeminent state during this period.

HAN DYNASTY

The Han dynasty ran from approximately 206 BC to AD 220. It began when a peasant, **Liu Pang**, led a successful insurrection against the Qin dynasty leaders. The **Han** shifted the capital of China to Changan (Xian). This was the period in which **Confucianism** became the dominant political and social ideology in China. The Han developed a code of laws and a form of government based upon the proper Confucian relations between king and subject, husband and wife, and father and son. The Han dynasty saw China accrue fantastic wealth and become one of the most sophisticated and resplendent countries the world has seen. Eventually, though, peasant revolts weakened the Han and made them susceptible to overthrow.

DAOISM

Next to Confucianism, **Daoism** (also Taoism) is the most important philosophy to have emerged out of China. **Taoist thought** is based on the 6th century-BC writings of **Lao Tzu**, specifically on the Tao Te Ching. Lao Tzu was a student of Confucius and taught that individuals should discover the essential nature of things and of themselves and should not seek to challenge the natural harmony of life. A proper Taoist should be patient and austere. Unlike Confucianism, Daoism contains an element of mysticism and so may be called a religion. Taoism introduced the concept of the **yin and yang**, the contrasting male and female elements that make up everything in existence and which must be harmonized in order to achieve self-realization.

EARLY CIVILIZATIONS OF MESOAMERICA AND SOUTH AMERICA

Mesoamerica, which is now known as Central and South America, were both host to developed civilizations 3,000 years before the arrival of Columbus. These civilizations were largely dependent upon water-supported agriculture. The most important crop in the region was **maize**. The first dominant group in this region, the **Olmecs**, was based in what is now the gulf coast of eastern Mexico. The Olmecs were known for making large and elaborate stone carvings. There were also major civilizations at this time in what is now Peru. In the Andes Mountains of that region, the **Chavin** culture developed intricate stone temples and pyramids. These sites have been explored carefully by archaeologists.

HINDUISM

Hinduism is the traditional religion of India. It is expressed in an individual's philosophy and behavior, rather than in the performance of any specific rituals. **Hinduism** does not claim a founder but has evolved slowly over thousands of years; the first Hindu writings date back to the third millennium BC. There are a few concepts that are common to all permutations of Hinduism, such as the **Vedas**, which are considered to be the sacred texts of the religion. The chief aim in life for a

Hindu is to be liberated from the cycle of suffering and rebirth. Hindus believe in **reincarnation** and that a person's conduct in this life will affect his or her position in the next (**karma**). Although Hinduism is frequently associated with the caste system, the two are actually unrelated.

Hindu Caste System

The Hindu caste system is a means of organizing society. It divides the populace into four groups, each associated with a part of the body of the Hindu god Purusha. The highest class is the **Brahmins**, associated with the mouth of the god. In the original system, the brahmin class was made up of priests. The second caste is the **Kshatriyas**, made up of rulers and soldiers; this caste is associated with the arms of Purusha. Next are the **Vaishyas**, associated with the legs of the god. This caste was composed of landowners, merchants, and artisans. The last group is the **Shudras**, associated with the feet of the god. This caste was composed of servants and slaves. Women do not have a place in the traditional Hindu caste system.

Judaism

Judaism was founded by **Abraham** in the 20th century BC. Abraham was called out from among the Chaldeans to enter into a covenant with God, whereby he and his descendants would receive special treatment and an inheritance of land. Abraham then moved to Canaan (near present-day Israel). Later, his descendants would move to Egypt and be enslaved. They were eventually liberated from slavery in Egypt by God through Moses, and they conquered the land of Canaan under the leadership of Joshua. Moses received from God a set of strict laws, the **Ten Commandments**; all of this is described in the **Torah**, the essential Jewish Scripture. There are also several other important books, including the Talmud, and many important commentaries by learned Jewish theologians.

Creation of Ancient Israel

Around the year 1020 BC, **Saul** became the first king of the Jewish nation, known as **Israel**. Saul's successor **David** conquered the city of Jerusalem and united all of the tribes of Israel, making Jerusalem their capital. In the 10th century BC, David's son **Solomon** built the first Jewish Temple in Jerusalem; this building was used to house the **Ark of the Covenant**, which housed the original Torah. Israel would be taken over by the **Assyrians** in the 8th century BC, and later by the **Babylonians**. Finally, in 538 BC, the Persian King Cyrus allowed the Jews to return to Jerusalem and rebuild the Temple. Israel would subsequently be taken over by the **Greeks** under Alexander, and later by the **Romans** under Pompey.

Vedic Age

The Vedic Age is the period recounted in the Indian Vedas, the earliest known records of Indian history. The dates of the **Vedic age** are considered by most to be between 2000 and 1000 BC. The oldest Vedic text is the **Rig-Veda**, which bears many Indo-Iranian elements. It is a collection of religious hymns and stories and describes a nomadic people who were ruled by a king who depended on their consent. His main duty was to protect the people. Religion in this period primarily consisted of chanting and the performing of sacrifices. During this period, elaborate rules concerning marriage were created, and the rigid social stratification that would become known as the **caste system** evolved.

Buddhism

Buddhism was created by **Gautama Siddhartha** (otherwise known as Buddha) in about 528 B.C. It was in part a response to Hinduism, which Buddha felt had become bloated with worldliness and politics. Traditional Buddhism is based upon the **Four Noble Truths**: existence is suffering, suffering is caused by desire, an end of suffering will come with Nirvana, and Nirvana will come with the practice of the **Eightfold Path**. The steps of the Eightfold Path are as follows: right views, right resolve, right speech, right action, right livelihood, right effort, right mindfulness, and right concentration. Buddhism has no deities. Buddhism did not receive any official sanction for a long time but did eventually spread and take hold in India, China, Japan, and elsewhere.

PERSIA

Persia is the European name for the region that is now Iran. This area has been the site of a number of vibrant cultures. The **Medes** were the first to develop there, lasting from approximately 700 to 549 BC, when they were expelled by the army of Cyrus. This great king then established the **Achaemenid dynasty**, which itself was destroyed by Alexander the Great in 330 BC. After this, a succession of peoples including the **Parthians**—rivals to Rome—inhabited the region, until a durable **Sasanian dynasty** was established in AD 224. Persia was in constant conflict with the **Byzantine Empire**, and would eventually be overtaken by the **Arabs** in the 7th century AD.

ZOROASTRIANISM

Zoroastrianism was the state religion of Persia during the **Sasanian dynasty** between the years AD 224 and 651. It is based upon the prophecies of **Zoroaster** (also known as Zarathustra, c. 628-551 BC), a Persian who claimed to have encountered the divine being Ahura Mazda. Zoroastrians believed that the world was composed of good and evil spirits, who are in constant conflict. Fire was sacred to the Zoroastrians. Many of the concepts of Zoroastrianism would be included in Christianity, especially by the Manichean sect, who also saw the world as a struggle between absolute good and absolute evil. Zoroastrianism receded in popularity with the rise of Islam.

CITY-STATE OF ATHENS IN ANCIENT GREECE

Ancient Greece was dominated by two city-states, **Athens** and **Sparta**. These two had very distinct cultures. Athens was a coastal city with a democratic form of government which amassed wealth by trading overseas. Athens is also known as the city that gave life to philosophy and the arts. **Socrates** engaged in his famous dialogues in the streets of Athens, and though he was eventually executed by the Athenian government for supposedly corrupting the youth, his thoughts achieved immortality in the writings of his student **Plato**. In turn, Plato's student **Aristotle** developed a strict form of reasoning that has formed the basis of much subsequent Western thought. Athens is also renowned for the architectural marvel that is the **Parthenon**.

SPARTA IN ANCIENT GREECE

While Athens was known for its devotion to the arts and its democratic form of government, its rival city-state **Sparta** was devoted to agriculture and the military. Sparta was not located on the coast, and therefore the Spartans had little contact with distant peoples. Spartan society was governed by a strict class system. Most people (**helots**) worked the land of other people as virtual serfs. In the upper classes, participation in **military training** was compulsory. Indeed, Spartan youths left their families to begin military training at a young age. The Spartans did not produce any noteworthy philosophers, but as a culture, they stressed the good of the group over that of the individual. This is in stark contrast to most Athenian thought, which celebrates the achievements of the individual.

> **Review Video: Ancient Greece**
> Visit mometrix.com/academy and enter code: 800829

GREECE IN THE PERICLEAN AND HELLENISTIC AGES

The **Periclean Age** in Greece, so named because Pericles was the leader of Athens during the period, took place in the 5th century BC. It was during this period that most of the great contributions to Western culture were made, including the philosophy of Socrates, the medical work of Hippocrates, and the great dramatic works of Aeschylus, Sophocles, and Euripides. The **Hellenistic Age** (4th century BC), on the other hand, is more commonly known for the military conquests made by **Alexander the Great**. If it were not for the conquests of Alexander during the Hellenistic Age, many of the innovations and achievements of the Periclean Age may not have had such a great influence on the West. It should be noted that the Hellenistic Age was not without its own great thinkers; in fact, Alexander studied as a boy under Aristotle.

MAJOR WARS OF GREECE IN THE PERICLEAN AND HELLENISTIC AGES

During the **Age of Pericles**, an alliance of Greek city-states was challenged by the mighty Persians. Miraculously, the outnumbered Greeks were able to defeat the Persians at Thermopylae and Marathon, and staved off conquest. The war with the Persians impoverished the Greeks, however, and increased rivalries among the city-states. In Athens, the requirements for citizenship were loosened, though slavery remained. Conflict between Sparta and Athens culminated in the **Peloponnesian War**, won by Sparta. Eventually, the whole of Greece would be conquered by **Philip of Macedon**, who allowed the Greeks to maintain their culture and traditions. **Alexander the Great** was the son of Philip and became the master of an empire larger than any the world had ever seen. During his reign, he united many disparate peoples through a common law and exchange policy. He died at the age of 33, and his empire was divided into three parts amongst his generals.

ROMAN REPUBLIC

Roman civilization dates from the founding of the city in 753 BC until the defeat of the last Emperor, **Romulus Augustus**, in AD 476. The republic itself lasted from the overthrow of the monarchy in 509 BC until the empowering of the first Emperor, **Octavian Augustus**, in 27 BC. The area along the Tiber River where Rome would be built was previously inhabited by a group known as the **Etruscans**. Rome took its name from the legendary **Romulus**, who is said to have founded it after triumphing over his brother Remus. The basic structure of Roman society consisted of **patricians** at the top of the social hierarchy, who were descendants of the founders of the republic and often wealthy. Beneath the patricians were the **plebeians**, which consisted of all other freemen. Finally, at the bottom of the social hierarchy were **slaves**. Women were not included in most social or economic business, although a Roman woman's rights were often significantly preferable to her contemporaries in other civilizations. The **Roman Republic**, which was the first political arrangement of Rome, was led by two consuls who were chosen annually. The **consuls** presided over the **Senate**, made up of a permanent group of those who had been previously elected to a high-ranking magistracy (originally primarily patrician in composition), and the **Assembly**, which was solely for the plebeians. Rome had extensive laws covering individual and property rights.

> **Review Video: Roman Republic Part One**
> Visit mometrix.com/academy and enter code: 360192
>
> **Review Video: Roman Republic Part Two**
> Visit mometrix.com/academy and enter code: 881514

EXPANSION OF ROME
PUNIC WARS

The first real challenge to the territorial expansion of Rome was the city of **Carthage**, located across the Mediterranean in North Africa. Carthage was founded by the Phoenicians. There were three major conflicts, known as the **Punic Wars**, fought between Rome and Carthage. Rome won the **First Punic War** and acquired Sicily in the process. The Carthaginian effort in the **Second Punic War** was led by Hannibal and included his famous crossing of the Alps. Hannibal was quite successful in

Italy, but a combination of a war of attrition throughout Italy and the counterattacks on Carthaginian holdings in Spain and the city of Carthage itself by the Romans forced Hannibal to retreat to North Africa to defend Carthage. In the **Third Punic War**, Rome finally destroyed Carthage; in fact, it is often rumored that the victorious Romans burned Carthage to the ground and then salted the fields of their vanquished foe, a tribute to the Senator Cato the Elder's repeated cry at the end of various speeches of *"Ceterum censeo Carthaginem esse delendam"* ("Moreover, I have determined that Carthage must be destroyed").

> **Review Video: The Punic Wars**
> Visit mometrix.com/academy and enter code: 879745

GREECE, GAUL, AND SPAIN

After defeating Carthage once and for all, Rome met little resistance as it continued to acquire more territory. This was partly due to the superiority of Roman weaponry, and in part because the Romans were good at bringing conquered peoples into the fold. Rome typically allowed conquered people to maintain their native cultures, so long as they paid tribute to Rome. Rome defeated the Macedonians and took **Greece**, then conquered large portions of **Gaul** (France) and **Spain**. The vastness of the Roman Empire necessitated some advances in infrastructure technology. Romans are justly famous for their solid and durable **roads** and **aqueducts** (systems for delivering water), many of which survive today.

GRAND ALLIANCE OF JULIUS CAESAR IN ROME

As Rome continued to expand, class conflicts developed between the nobility and the poor. In this era of unrest, it became possible for individual leaders to claim more power than the law had allowed previously. In 60 B.C., the famous general Julius Caesar formed the three-person alliance known as the First Triumvirate to govern Rome. The other two members were **Gnaeus Pompey Magnus** and **Marcus Licinius Crassus**. During this period, Caesar led a successful campaign against the Gauls (a people in modern-day France) and made himself richer than the entire Roman State on the proceeds from his conquest. After Crassus was killed in battle, Caesar pushed Pompey out and assumed total control of Rome, crowning himself dictator-for-life. Though Caesar was very popular with the mob, his decision to claim lifelong power alienated him from the nobility in the Senate. He was assassinated by a group of senators, led by **Marcus Iunius Brutus**, in 44 B.C.

SECOND ROMAN TRIUMVIRATE

After the assassination of Caesar in 44 B.C., Rome was mired in chaos. Those who had conspired to kill Caesar had hoped to return to the republican form of government, but instead another trio of leaders came to the fore, this time as a governmental commission of "three men for reconstituting the Republic," known as the **Triumvirate**. The Triumvirate was composed of **Marc Antony**, one of Caesar's greatest generals and a Consul at the time; **Octavius**, the nephew and testamentary heir of Caesar; and **Marcus Aemilius Lepidus**, a third wheel who was quickly made a non-entity. While Octavius stayed in Rome, Antony left for Egypt, where he stayed for a time as the guest and lover of **Cleopatra**. Eventually, infighting between Octavius and Antony led the former to mount a campaign against Egypt. When they realized that they were defeated, Antony and Cleopatra committed suicide to avoid the shame of being paraded in Octavian's triumph. Lepidus having been marginalized, Octavius (now known as Augustus) became the first **Emperor**.

PAX ROMANA

After the ascension of Augustus, Rome entered a period of relative tranquility. Augustus dubbed this era, which lasted about forty years, the **Pax Romana**. Rome remained an empire, although the conquered peoples were able to obtain Roman citizenship without having to forfeit their native customs. It was at this period that Rome reached its greatest geographic proportions, stretching all the way up to present-day Scotland. This was also the greatest period for **Roman artistic achievement**; both Virgil and Ovid were active during the Pax Romana, and, indeed, the Aeneid of Virgil was written in part to glorify Augustus. It was at this time that the polytheist religion of Rome was challenged first by the **Judaism** of the conquered Hebrews, and later by the early **Christians**.

CONSTANTINE AND THE CHRISTIANS

The Roman Emperor **Constantine**, in response to the inconvenient vastness of his dominion, established an eastern capital: **Constantinople**, in AD 330. Having received a sign in the heavens which promised him victory over his rivals for the office of Emperor should he convert to Christianity, Constantine famously issued the **Edict of Milan**, in which he called for the end of the persecution of Christians, after a sound victory as promised. After this act, Christianity flourished in the Roman Empire and became the official religion of the state. A movement called **monasticism** developed within the religion, advocating the renunciation of worldly goods in favor of contemplation and prayer. After the death of Constantine, the empire once again proved unwieldy for one man, and therefore it split as it had previously, with the western half being governed from Rome and the eastern half from Constantinople. This arrangement would prove untenable, however; a Germanic tribe of **barbarians** eventually sacked Rome, and the western Roman capital fell in AD 476.

BYZANTINE EMPIRE

The eastern half of the Roman Empire became known as the **Byzantine Empire**. After the fall of Rome, **Emperor Justinian** led successfully from Constantinople for a number of years. The Justinian era is especially remembered for the contributions to law and religious artwork, in particular the development of mosaics. In the years after the fall of Rome, the **Catholic Christian Church** gradually rose to fill the power vacuum. In what had been the Western Roman Empire, the Church acted completely independent of any political body, while even in the Byzantine Empire the Church was increasing in power. Only the influence of the Byzantine Emperor kept the Church from being the most powerful group in all of Europe.

RISE OF CHRISTIANITY

Early Christianity was a mass of competing doctrines, including various groups such as the Gnostics and Arians who all sought to have their view legitimized as the truth. Eventually, the **orthodox church**, through an ecumenical council of bishops, created in the 4th century AD the canon of New Testament texts which exists today. The apostles had created a hierarchy of bishops, priests, and deacons who stressed obedience to duly constituted church authority. By the middle of the 2nd century, Christianity began to attract intellectuals in the **Roman Empire**. Although Christians were still liable to be persecuted in the farther reaches of the empire, many turned to the Church as the empire crumbled, as the Church was all that was left of civilization, and would rebuild Europe over the next millennium.

KINGDOM OF KUSH

Kush was a powerful African kingdom that lasted in some form from 2000 BC until AD 350. For a long time, **Kush** was based around the city of **Kerma**, in what is now Sudan. Kushites became wealthy because of their mineral resources and because of their advantageous location in the northwest corner of Africa, where they were at the crossroads of several intercontinental trade routes. There was a great deal of contact between Kush and **Egypt** in this period. In 767 BC, King Kashta of Kush defeated the Egyptians, and the Kushites had control of the entire Nile Valley. Kush would soon be weakened by the Assyrians, however, and would eventually fall prey to the **Romans**; in AD 350, the new capital of Kush, Meroe, was sacked.

Aksum (Axum)

Aksum, a town in what is now northern Ethiopia, was the capital city of one of Africa's most powerful kingdoms between the 1st and 6th centuries AD. The kings of **Aksum** were said to have descended from **Menelik**, one of the sons of the famous King Solomon. These people controlled almost all of the trade on the **Red Sea** and made a tremendous profit on the exchange of ivory. In the 4th century AD, Aksum eliminated the kingdom of **Kush** and became the predominant power in Africa. It was also during this century that Aksum was **Christianized**; it remains a hub of Ethiopian Christianity to this day. In its later stages, Aksum's control extended into southern Arabia and would eventually give way to the Persians and the Arabs.

Nok Culture

One of the most successful cultures of the African Iron Age was the **Nok culture**. The Nok developed **ironworking** technology before anyone else, and also created a rich artistic culture that spread throughout the West African forest region. The Nok were mainly active between the 5th and the 1st centuries BC. Their creation of iron farm implements made it possible for farmers to develop surplus crops, and thus urban centers could develop. This increase in agricultural productivity also made it possible for there to be more specialization of labor. Therefore, not only were civilizations more stable, but they were also better able to protect themselves, as they now had both better weapons made of iron and more time to train warriors.

Ancient Ghana

Beginning in the 7th century AD, **Ghana** was a major trading power in west Africa. It was mainly located in the areas that are now known as Mali and Mauritania. The people of Ghana grew rich by exchanging ivory and gold from the south and salt from the north. Eventually, Ghana would become an empire and would collect lavish tributes from all of the lands within its control. In the 11th century, the capital of Ghana was **Kumbi**. In 1076, however, Kumbi fell to the Almoravids, a Muslim tribe. The whole of Ghana would eventually be subsumed into the burgeoning empire of **Mali**.

Ancient Mali

Today, Mali is the largest nation in West Africa. Indeed, throughout African history, **Mali** has been a major power. Until the 11th century, it was a part of the empire of Ghana, a wealthy trading nation. Mali would eventually rise to prominence in its own right. The economy of Mali was based upon the rich mineral resources (especially gold) of the region. Mali reached its highest prominence during the reign of **Mansa Musa** (AD 1312-7). This ruler introduced Islam to his people, which at this time lived as far north as Morocco. The city of **Timbuktu** became a cultural center for the region, as well as a crossroads for trade routes that stretched across the Sahara. Over time, internal disputes would divide Mali into several smaller kingdoms.

Songhai Empire

The Songhai empire flourished in West Africa between the 14th and 16th centuries. Centered in the valley of the Niger River, the **Songhai** were first organized by Christian **Berbers** in the 7th century. Four hundred years later, they established their capital at **Gao** and became an Islamic nation. Except for a brief period in which they were ruled by the empire of Mali, the Songhai controlled over a thousand miles along the Niger. Like most of the African powers, the Songhai made their money through trade. **Muhammad I**, who ruled from 1493 to 1528, expanded the empire to its greatest area. One of the weaknesses of the Songhai, however, was that they did not have a traditional means of succession, and thus frequent infighting among the powerful eventually led to the empire's demise.

THE HUNS

The Huns were a nomadic people who moved east across central Asia during the 4th century AD. The **Huns** were divided into several branches. The **White Huns** overran the Sasanian Empire and conquered many cities in the northern part of the Indian subcontinent. Another group roamed eastern Europe and established a strong empire on the Hungarian Plain around AD 400. The Huns were known for their amazing horsemanship and for being aggressive on the battlefield. It was under the guidance of **Attila** (440s) that the Huns reached their highest level of prominence. During this period, they collected tribute from many of the areas within the Roman Empire. Soon after the death of Attila, however, the Huns became complacent and lost most of their territory.

THE MONGOLS

The Mongols, who descended from the Huns, were a nomadic group that roamed east-central Asia. Around the year AD 1206, the various **Mongol** tribes were united under **Genghis Khan**, whose empire then stretched from the Black Sea to the Pacific Ocean, and from Tibet to Siberia. After the death of Genghis, the Mongol lands were divided up. This did not, however, slow expansion; Mongols eventually controlled parts of Iran as well. **Kublai Khan** was another prominent Mongol leader; he destroyed the Song dynasty in China and replaced it with the Yuan. By the 14th century, the Mongol Empire was beginning to disintegrate. Like many of its kind, it proved too large to govern. The Ming and subsequently the Qing dynasties put the remaining Mongols under Chinese control.

EMERGENCE OF RUSSIA

In the Middle Ages, Russia had a complicated and inefficient system of succession, which meant that the various lands were constantly being fought over, and authority was often dubious. For a long time, **Russia** was dominated by the **Mongols** (Tatars), who kept the local governments weak in order to continue receiving tributes. Moscow was able to parlay loyalty to the Tatars and colonization of other feudal estates into a great deal of power during this period. Supported by their Tatar overlords, the **Muscovite princes** were able to partition off their new lands in such a way that it became very difficult for nobles to consolidate their landholdings, which prevented any wealthy lords from ever challenging the princes of Moscow.

STEPPE PEOPLES AND SELJUK TURKS

Between the years AD 1000 and 1450, invaders from the **steppes** conquered parts of Asia, the Middle East, and Europe. These people had originally been nomads, but in this period, they began to settle and become tradesmen. The clans that made up this group were loosely based on family ties; once they became stationary, they began to appoint powerful chiefs for leadership support. Near AD 1000, the **Seljuk Turks** moved from Central Asia into the Middle East. This group then controlled the trade routes between Asia, Africa, and Europe, and charged tolls on these routes, building an empire with their wealth. In 1071, the Seljuk Turks defeated the Byzantines at the **Battle of Manzikert**; a Christian defeat which would be part of the motivation for the **First Crusade**. The Seljuk Turks were known as excellent fighters and mediocre rulers; local leaders frequently ignored the central government and fought one another for control of land. This infighting weakened the group until they became prey to new nomadic invaders from Central Asia.

POLAND AND HUNGARY IN EASTERN EUROPE DURING THE MIDDLE AGES

During the Middle Ages, a number of different leaders tried to unite the various lands of **Poland**. These attempts were always defeated by the nobility, who preferred the country to be an oligarchy rather than a monarchy. Poland was also much involved during this period in a battle with the **Teutonic knights** over the Baltic coastline. **Hungary** was a feudal state by the beginning of the

14th century, and the various patches of land which constituted the country were ruled as if they were independent. Bishops in the **Eastern Orthodox Church** were among the largest landholders. Ostensibly, the nobility was in charge of the defense of the Hungarian people, though they rarely supplied the money and material for war.

ORIGINS AND EXPANSION OF ISLAM

The religion of Islam was founded by the prophet **Muhammad** in AD 610. **Islam** is a monotheistic religion based on the **Koran**, a book of scripture according to the Muslim god, **Allah**. The practice of Islam is based on "**Five Pillars**": faith in Allah, a pilgrimage to the city of Mecca, a yearly fast during the month of Ramadan, the giving of alms, and prayer five times a day. Muhammad also asserted that Islam should be spread throughout the world. Indeed, as the Christian Church was becoming the dominant factor in Europe, Islam was spreading throughout North Africa, the Middle East, parts of Asia, and even Spain. The simultaneous ascensions of Christianity and Islam inevitably led to conflict, most notably in the **Crusades**.

> **Review Video: Islam**
> Visit mometrix.com/academy and enter code: 359164

ISLAMIC CIVILIZATION

After the formation of Islam in the 7th century AD, it took 3 or 4 centuries to develop the institutional structures of the religion. **Islamic law** was created, and a new class of Muslim religious leaders and scholars emerged who took a prominent place in society. The Islamic civilization drew elements from its surroundings, namely the culture of the Greeks, Iranians, Christians, Jews, and Zoroastrians. At first, the Islamic Empire was ruled by a single **caliph** and a small Arab elite. As the empire expanded, however, this became untenable, and the lands were divided into a number of independent political entities. Also, factions began to emerge among Muslims, most notably between the **Sunnis** and **Shiites**, who rivaled over the true successor to Muhammad, among other issues. Because the entire Islamic world operated with a common system of trade, it quickly became very wealthy.

> **Review Video: The Islamic Empire**
> Visit mometrix.com/academy and enter code: 511181

FEUDALISM IN WESTERN EUROPE

Feudalism was the system of social and economic organization that developed in Europe in the Middle Ages (roughly AD 750 to 1300). **Feudalism** is characterized by rigid hierarchies among the various classes. At the top of the hierarchy was the **king**, and below him **lords**, who oversaw a smaller area of land. Below the lords were **noblemen** who had been granted control over farmland in exchange for their pledge of allegiance to the king. These noblemen were known as **vassals** and **subvassals**. The land managed by each vassal was known as a **fief**, and the home of the vassal was known as the **manor**. Each manor and the community surrounding it comprised a self-sufficient unit. The laws of **primogeniture** were enforced at this time, meaning that the ownership of the fief would descend to the firstborn son of the lord. Finally, the land was cultivated either by **peasants** or **serfs**; peasants were free farmers, while serfs were basically slaves who were forced to work for the lord and were bound to their lands.

CHARLEMAGNE

The emergence of the feudal system in Western Europe meant that instead of a centralized power, there were many local authorities. **Charlemagne** (AD 742-814) was a Germanic leader who tried to unify the former Western Roman Empire. In AD 800, **Pope St. Leo III** crowned Charlemagne

Emperor of Rome during Christmas Mass at St. Peter's Basilica in Rome, establishing a political relationship with the **Church** that would last throughout the Middle Ages. Charlemagne allocated a great deal of power to regional leaders and did not tax his subjects. For this reason, he was unable to make many internal improvements during his reign. Nevertheless, Charlemagne is credited with promoting the arts, especially within the thriving monasteries, without which much of antiquity would not have been transcribed and thus preserved. After the death of Charlemagne, his lands were divided up among his three grandsons according to the **Treaty of Verdun**.

HOLY ROMAN EMPIRE

The Holy Roman Empire was the name given to the holdings of **Otto the Great** in 962, who had unified the central area of Charlemagne's empire. As in Charlemagne's day, this was a disparate group of territories, and proved difficult to govern. Otto incorporated the **Church** into his government, though he continually sought to minimize its power. One of the legacies of Otto's reign would be the rivalry between the Church and state. Gradually, the Church leaders acquired power, until they were exercising great control over the day-to-day activities of most citizens. Perhaps inevitably, this great power began to corrupt many of the Church's leaders. Indicative of the state of the Church was the often unpunished offense of **simony**, in which prestigious and important offices were bought and sold.

> **Review Video: The Middle Ages: The Holy Roman Empire**
> Visit mometrix.com/academy and enter code: 137655

WESTERN EUROPE IN THE 12TH AND 13TH CENTURIES

In the 12th century AD, the various **fiefs** in Western Europe increasingly came into contact with one another. As advances in transportation technology made trade with distant neighbors possible, there developed more necessity for specialization. Rather than be entirely self-sufficient, lords found it was more economically advantageous to perfect the cultivation of one crop and exchange that for everything else. As **trade** became more important, so did the merchants in towns, known as burghers, who wielded considerable political power. Trade arrangements led to alliances between various towns, and the whole of Western Europe became more homogenous. The distinction between **classes** also became much less pronounced during this period. There were drawbacks, however: the increasing number of people in towns, as well as the more frequent travel between towns, contributed, no doubt, to the **bubonic plague epidemic** of the mid-14th century.

FAITH AND LEARNING IN WESTERN EUROPE DURING THE LATE MIDDLE AGES

Surprising though it may seem, one of the best things that happened to Christian thought during the Middle Ages was its contact with **Islam**. The complex philosophies of Muslim scholars helped spur the evolution of **Christian theology**. These, in addition to the rediscovery of ancient philosophers such as Aristotle, led Christians to begin to glorify **reason** as the God-given tool for investigating religious faith. Many assertions made by the new rational theologians, however, were dubbed **heresy** by many Church leaders, as more and more Christian thinkers were bemoaning the materialistic ways of the Church leaders. One of the leading Christian thinkers of the Middle Ages was **St. Thomas Aquinas**, whose *Summa Theologica* outlined rational explanations for the belief in God and in the miracles of Christianity.

FORMATION OF UNIVERSITIES IN THE MIDDLE AGES

The rapid evolution in Christian thought that took place during the Middle Ages gave rise to the formation of the first **universities**. For the first time in Western Europe, young men would move to large cities to study theology, law, and medicine at formal institutions. In addition to this trend, the academic method known as **scholasticism** was developed, in which scholars would use logic and deductive reasoning in order to analyze a work or determine something of an abstract nature. Among the so-called scholastics, two schools of thought developed: those scholars who adhered to the ideas of Plato were known as **realists**, and those who followed Aristotle were known as **nominalists**. The word *realist* is somewhat confusing when used to refer to the work of Plato, who believed that our perceptions of objects were merely perceptions of the barest shadows of their reality. Another development of Christianity in this period was **mysticism**; Christian mystics believed that they could achieve union with God through self-denial, contemplative prayer, and alms-giving.

GERMANY, ITALY, AND FRANCE IN THE 13TH CENTURY

During the 13th century, France was transformed from a group of disparate fiefs into a centralized monarchy by **Philip Augustus** (Philip II). His heir, Philip IV, would establish the **Estates General**, a governing body composed of representatives from each province. The Estates General contained noblemen as well as wealthy commoners. Meanwhile, Germany endured an **interregnum**, or period between kings, after the ruler died without a clear successor. Italy, as well, spent this period as a collection of strong and independent townships. In a decentralized state, it became easier for wealthy merchants to wield power. In Germany, the **Hanseatic League**, an association of merchants, set regional trade policy.

MAGNA CARTA

England, unlike many of the other regions of Western Europe, had been accustomed to a strong monarchy. This tradition was challenged in AD 1215, when noblemen forced King John to sign the **Magna Carta**, a document which gave feudal rights back to the nobles and extended the rule of law to the middle-class burghers. The Magna Carta made the formation of the **Houses of Parliament** possible. Over time, Parliament would evolve into a two-house structure: the **House of Lords**, which contained nobles and clergy, and the **House of Commons,** which contained knights and burghers. The House of Lords was mainly occupied with legal questions, while the House of Commons dealt mainly in economic issues.

FEUDALISM END IN WESTERN EUROPE

In the late 13th century, increased contact between regions and greater representation in government culminated in a number of **peasant revolts** and **serf uprisings**. During this period, members of the clergy became even more secular and open in their greed for fame and power. This alienated many common citizens from the Church. The invention of **gunpowder** also changed the social arrangements in Western Europe; fewer noblemen were willing to participate in combat, and so the code of chivalry gave way to **mercenary soldiers**. Noblemen largely turned their attention to acquiring some of the fantastic wealth available in trade. The quality that men strived for in these days was called **virtue**, meaning a solemn dedication to the arts and sciences.

PAPAL BULL "UNAM SANCTAM" AND THE CRISIS IN THE WESTERN CHURCH

Around the year 1300, the power of the Pope in political affairs was weakening because of the rise of strong monarchs and a spirit of nationalism. **Pope Boniface VIII** attempted to force kings to obey him but was unsuccessful. In response, Boniface issued a papal bull in 1296 that instructed **King Philip IV** of France to not tax the church; Philip ignored this command. Boniface would not relent, and issued the bull "**Unam Sanctam**," in which he declared that there are two powers on the earth, the temporal and the spiritual, with the latter always superior, and that there is no salvation outside of loyalty to the Roman Pontiff. Once again, Philip refused the claims of the Pope and decided to silence him by having him kidnapped and brought to France. Boniface was able to escape captivity but died soon afterward. This significantly weakened the political authority of the papacy.

BABYLON CAPTIVITY AND SCHISM AND THE CRISIS IN THE WESTERN CHURCH

After the death of Pope Boniface VIII, King Philip IV of France persuaded the College of Cardinals to select a French archbishop as the next pope. This pope, **Clement V**, moved the papacy to Avignon, France, where it would remain for 67 years. Debate raged during this period as to whether a pope could be legitimate in any city other than Rome. Also, Clement's court became notorious for its extravagance. In 1378, a new pope was chosen; an Italian, who chose the name **Urban VI** to indicate that he planned on keeping the papacy in Rome. Upset with Urban's policy, 13 French cardinals selected a new pope, the French-speaking **Clement VII**. Now, there were two popes, and each one declared the other illegitimate. This confusion lasted from 1378 until 1417, with the Pope in Rome and an antipope in Avignon.

HUNDRED YEARS' WAR

England made a claim on the French throne in 1337, and the result was a **war** (or series of wars) that lasted for 116 years. France was angry, in return, that England had not upheld its feudal obligations to the French throne, to whom the English king was technically a distant vassal. France had the support of the Pope, but England used the innovation of the longbow to score some significant victories. It was during this war that the charismatic figure **Joan of Arc** emerged. Joan was a French peasant who led troops to several unlikely victories after being visited by God. Her deeds rallied the spirits of the French, and France eventually won. The catastrophic losses suffered by both sides had major consequences: England withdrew from contention as a land power, electing instead to develop a **navy**; in France, **Louis IX**—St. Louis—took advantage of the chaos to consolidate power in the monarchy.

EFFECTS OF THE BLACK DEATH AND JOHANNES GUTENBERG

Toward the end of the Middle Ages, two events greatly shaped future events. The **bubonic plague**, also known as the Black Death, killed between 30% and 60% of the European population. The influx of people to squalid cities made the rapid spread of this disease possible. The seemingly random devastation caused by the disease caused many people to question their faith, and the power of the Church suffered as a result. The other monumental event was the invention of the **printing press** by Johannes Gutenberg in about 1436. This invention was used first to produce a cheap copy of the Bible. Soon, though, printing presses with movable type were being used to print all sorts of things, and the literacy rate in Europe rose dramatically. It immediately became possible to disseminate ideas quickly.

> **Review Video: An Overview of the Black Death**
> Visit mometrix.com/academy and enter code: 431857

FEUDALISM IN JAPAN

Feudalism developed in Japan after wars in the 11th century left much of the land in the control of military leaders. These men did not actually own the land, but a complex set of rights were given to them, whereby they had the exclusive right to cultivate and profit from the land. Many Japanese were disenchanted with the central government at this time, so the idea of powerful regional leaders appealed to them. A code of ethics specific to feudalism emerged, and Japanese peasants were required to pledge loyalty to a particular lord rather than to a political ideal. One particular feudal administration, the **Minamoto**, acquired almost the entirety of Japan and replaced the central government for most people.

MAYAS

The Mayas were based in Mexico's Yucatan Peninsula, Tabasco, and Chiapas, as well as in what is now Guatemala and Honduras. Between the years AD 200 and 950, they developed a sophisticated civilization, with complex religions, architecture, arts, engineering, and astronomy. The **Mayas** did have a form of hieroglyphic writing, but most of their history and folklore was preserved orally. The Mayas are responsible for creating an extremely accurate **calendar** and for first conceiving the number **zero**. The Maya civilization was supported by agriculture, but it was run by a class of priests and warriors. In the 9th century, the Mayas were overrun by Toltecs from the north, who created the legend of the feathered serpent **Quetzalcoatl**.

MAYA RELIGION

The Mayas conceived of the universe as a flat, square earth, whose four corners and center were dominated by a god. Above the sky, there were 13 levels, and below were 9 underworlds, each dominated by a god. The sun and moon, deities in their own right, passed through all of these levels every day. Each male god had a female goddess counterpart. The Mayas also had patron gods and goddesses for various occupations and classes. Maya rulers had religious powers. Religious rituals often entailed human sacrifice and self-mutilation. The Mayas also played a ritual ball game that had religious importance; the losers of this game stood to lose their lives. Mayas developed their cities as tributes to the gods.

AZTECS

When the **Toltec empire** had been eradicated around the year 1150, the power in Mesoamerica shifted to the valley of Mexico, around three lakes. By about 1325, the **Aztecs** had seized control of this area. The Aztec civilization was organized into **city-states**, much like early medieval Europe; political intrigue and state marriages were as common among the Aztecs as among the French. The Aztecs were known as fierce warriors and were hated by their neighbors because of their brutality. According to legend, the Aztecs settled in **Tenochtitlan** after a scout saw an eagle with a serpent in its beak perched on a cactus there. The Aztecs formed alliances based on threats and forced tributes.

INCAS

The Incas inhabited a huge area, from present-day Ecuador to central Chile to the eastern side of the Andes Mountains. The **Incas'** territory expanded especially after the 14th century AD. The Incas were engaged in frequent conflicts with rival groups, and they frequently enslaved the groups that they defeated. They eventually formed a permanent underclass of **serfs** in order to ensure that the lands of the military leaders would be cultivated. Incas typically dispersed rival groups in order to prevent being attacked. The Incan religion contained a god in heaven, a cult of ancestors, and a number of sacred objects and places. The Incas called themselves the **children of the Sun**.

TANG DYNASTY

The Tang dynasty was in control of China from AD 618 to 907. One of the main projects pursued by the **Tang** rulers was the **unification** of the far-flung and diverse Chinese states. The early portion of the Tang dynasty is considered one of the high points in Chinese history; the economy and the arts both flourished. Under the leadership of Tang generals, Chinese soldiers would claim parts of Afghanistan, Tibet, and Korea. The Tang were also somewhat unique as Chinese leaders in that they encouraged the introduction of foreign ideas into Chinese culture. **Printing** was invented in China during this period, and thus ideas could be disseminated much more easily. The end of the Tang dynasty came after a period of internal governmental conflict.

Song Dynasty

The Song dynasty of China lasted between the years AD 960 and 1279. The **Song** rulers are credited with reuniting many portions of China that had become disjointed. Historians usually distinguish between the Northern and the Southern Song. The leaders of the Song dynasty made a deliberate effort to reduce the emphasis on military conquest; instead, they focused on developing China's **civil service**. The Song dynasty saw a rejuvenation of **Confucian philosophy** in China, as well as a renewed interest in the **arts**. Some people compare the Song dynasty with the European Renaissance. The Song was the only dynasty in China not to be ended by internal conflict; the Song were ousted by a rebel leader instead.

Mauryan Empire

The Mauryan Empire lasted approximately between the years 321 and 185 BC. in India. It was established by the powerful leader **Chandragupta Maurya** and featured a strong military and an efficient bureaucracy. The **Mauryan empire** eventually spread as far west of the Indus River as present-day Afghanistan. At its greatest expansion, the Mauryan empire comprised almost the entirety of what is now India. The leader **Ashoka** (c. 272-232 BC) converted to Buddhism, and his rule was prosperous for rich and poor alike. After the death of Ashoka, however, the Mauryan Empire splintered, as the southern lands sought autonomy and the northern lands were subject to constant foreign invasions.

Chapter Quiz

Ready to see how well you retained what you just read? Scan the QR code to go directly to the chapter quiz interface for this study guide. If you're using a computer, simply visit the online resources page at **mometrix.com/resources719/apworldhistory-27797** and click the Chapter Quizzes link.

World History: 1400 to 1914

Transform passive reading into active learning! After immersing yourself in this chapter, put your comprehension to the test by taking a quiz. The insights you gained will stay with you longer this way. Scan the QR code to go directly to the chapter quiz interface for this study guide. If you're using a computer, simply visit the online resources page at **mometrix.com/resources719/apworldhistory-27797** and click the Chapter Quizzes link.

BEGINNING OF THE RENAISSANCE

In the 14th century, the turmoil caused by war and plague weakened the power of Christian theology. In its place came the philosophy of **humanism**, in which the emphasis is placed on individual potential and determination while detracting from one's attention to the realm of the divine. Humanist thought contributed to a resurgence in the arts and sciences, which eventually came to be known as the **Renaissance**. In the 14th and 15th centuries, the center of this resurgence was in **Northern Italy**, in large part because this was the crossroads of several important trade routes. Specifically, the city-states of Milan, Florence, and Venice cultivated excellent artists. Talented youths typically studied in these cities with their expenses paid by a wealthy patron; the most famous patrons were the **Medici** family in Florence.

> **Review Video: The Renaissance**
> Visit mometrix.com/academy and enter code: 123100

ITALIAN ARTISTS OF THE RENAISSANCE

The early part of the Renaissance was dominated by the artists congregated in Northern Italy. Among them were several immortal talents. **Donatello** (1386-1466) sculpted a marvelous statue of David and was the first artist in this period to depict the naked human body (religious concerns had kept recent artists from doing so). **Botticelli** (1444-1510) is the painter of the famous Birth of Venus. **Leonardo da Vinci** (1452-1519) excelled in a number of different fields, but he is perhaps best known for painting the Mona Lisa and the Last Supper. **Michelangelo** (1475-1563), though, was probably the most famous painter and sculptor of the time; he painted the ceiling in the Sistine Chapel and sculpted the most famous statue of David.

LITERATURE AND SCIENCE IN THE RENAISSANCE

Although the Renaissance is typically associated with achievements in visual art, the period also saw a magnificent outpouring of literary and scientific talent. One of the most significant works to emerge from this period was *The Prince*, by the Florentine **Niccolo Macchiavelli**. This book outlined a practical plan for political management, one that would be emulated by ruthless leaders in the future. Some of the other noteworthy authors were **Erasmus** (*In Praise of Folly*), **Sir Thomas More** (*Utopia*), **Montaigne**, **Cervantes** (*Don Quixote*), **Ben Johnson**, **Christopher Marlowe**, and, of course, **William Shakespeare**. At the same time, remarkable advances were being made in the sciences. **Copernicus** incited controversy by suggesting that the Earth revolved around the Sun; **Kepler** and **Galileo** would acquire hard data to support this claim.

AGE OF EXPLORATION

The Age of Exploration is also called the **Age of Discovery**. It is generally considered to have begun in the early 15th century and continued into the 17th century. Major developments of the Age of

Exploration included **technological advances** in navigation, mapmaking, and shipbuilding. These advances led to expanded European exploration of the rest of the world. **Explorers** set out from several European countries, including Portugal, Spain, France, and England, seeking new routes to Asia. These efforts led to the discovery of new lands, as well as **colonization** in India, Asia, Africa, and North America.

> **Review Video: Age of Exploration**
> Visit mometrix.com/academy and enter code: 612972

ROLE OF ECONOMICS IN THE AGE OF EXPLORATION

At the same time that the Renaissance was reinvigorating European cultural life, a desire to explore the world abroad was growing. Indeed, the ability to make long voyages was facilitated by the advances in **navigational technology** made around this time. The main reason for exploration, though, was **economic**. Europeans had first been introduced to eastern goods during the Crusades, and the exploits of Marco Polo in the 13th century had further whetted the western appetite for contact with distant lands. This increasing focus on exploration and trade caused a general shift in the balance of power in Europe. Landlocked countries, like Germany, found that they were excluded from participating in the lucrative new economy. On the other hand, those countries which bordered the **Atlantic** (England, France, Spain, and Portugal) were the most powerful players.

OBSTACLES TO EXPLORATION BY EUROPE BEFORE 1400

Before 1400, few Europeans knew anything about the world. When **Christopher Columbus** read of the exploits of the Italian Marco Polo, however, he was inspired to seek out new trade routes. Also, **Prince Henry** of Portugal established a navigation institute that encouraged sailors to explore. For a long time, extended sea voyages were restricted by a lack of navigational and seafaring technology; the inventions of the compass, astrolabe, and caravel remedied this situation. There was also a high cost associated with long travels (around 1400); however, new monarchs in France, England, Spain, and Portugal decided that they were willing to pay a high price to get a piece of the spice trade. Finally, the question of a motive for exploration was answered by the increasing fervor for missionary work, as well as the economic necessity of developing new trade routes.

MAJOR EUROPEAN EXPLORERS

Vasco da Gama was the first European to sail around the Cape of Good Hope, on the southern tip of what is now South Africa. This made it possible to reach Asia by boat. **Balboa** explored Central America and was the first European to view the Pacific Ocean. **Magellan** is remembered as the first to circumnavigate the globe. **Cortes** was a powerful commander who subjugated the Aztecs in what is now Mexico; he used great brutality to achieve his ends. **Pizarro**, like Cortes, was a conquistador; he conquered the Incas in what is now Peru. **Amerigo Vespucci**, from whose name the word *America* was derived, mapped the Atlantic coast of South America and was able to convince stubborn Europeans that these lands were not a part of India.

JOINT-STOCK COMPANIES AT THE TIME OF THE AGE OF EXPLORATION

As exploration created new opportunities for amassing wealth, **Portugal** enjoyed special favor because of its excellent location and cordial relations with many of the Muslim nations of North Africa. The ruler of Portugal at this time was even known as Prince Henry "the Navigator" (1394-1460). In order to solidify trade arrangements, European rulers began to think about colonizing foreign lands. In order to fund these expensive trips, a new kind of business known as the **joint-stock company** was developed. In a joint-stock company, a group of merchants would combine their resources to pay for the passage of a vessel. These groups would later be influential in securing colonial charters for many of their agents. One of the most powerful examples was the **Muscovy Company of England**, which controlled almost all trade with Russia.

MERCANTILISM AT THE TIME OF THE AGE OF EXPLORATION

As foreign trade became the most important part of every nation's economy, the economic theory of **mercantilism** became popular. According to mercantilism, a nation should never import more than it exports. Of course, it is impossible for every country to achieve this goal at the same time, so European countries were in fierce competition at all times. The solution that most nations pursued was to establish **colonies**, because these could supply resources for export by the mother country without really being considered imports. This rush to colonize had disastrous consequences for the indigenous peoples of the Americas and Africa. Europeans often looted the Native Americans for anything of value, and their need for cheap labor to cultivate the land there spawned the **African slave trade**.

REFORMATION

A response to corruption in the Catholic Church and lapses in enforcement of the basic tenets of the faith, such as those against simony, the **Reformation** was a movement that called for a return to what many believed to be a simpler message of salvation that they felt to be more scripturally accurate. Many people in this time were outraged by the vast landholdings and stuffed coffers of the Church, which they felt should be concerned with tending to the spiritual health of its members. In 1440, the invention of the **printing press** had made it possible for ideas to be disseminated more widely, and authors of the Renaissance had sharply criticized the greed of the clergy. People were also angered by the selling of **ecclesial offices** and especially the selling of **indulgences**, in which a person would pay money to have one's time in purgatory shortened. Selling salvation was indeed against the tenets of the Church, but was often largely unenforced. The general distrust of the Church in this period is known as **anticlericalism**.

MARTIN LUTHER

Martin Luther was a German friar who first became famous for criticizing the Catholic Church's sale of indulgences. In **1517**, in accordance with the tradition of theological debate, **Luther** posted his critique of this practice on the door of his local church; the document known as the "**Ninety-five Theses**" won him immediate fame. Luther then set about undermining the institution of the Church, arguing that individuals did not need the help of clergy to establish a strong relationship with God. Luther went even further, stating that faith, rather than obedience to arbitrary Church rules, would be what got individuals into heaven. The final straw for the Church came when Luther directly challenged the Pope, declaring that no one man could be the perfect interpreter of Scripture. Luther was excommunicated but continued to spread his message. Germany was then wracked by a war between the Lutherans of the north and the Catholics of the south. The **Peace of Augsburg** in 1555 was the resolution to this conflict, in which the subjects of a prince would follow that prince's faith, a practice referred to as *cuius regio, cuius religio*—literally, "whose jurisdiction, whose religion."

> **Review Video: Martin Luther and the Reformation**
> Visit mometrix.com/academy and enter code: 691828

PROTESTANTS

Inspired by Luther, many other critics of Catholic excess joined together throughout Europe. These groups were known collectively as **Protestants**. One of the largest sects of Protestants was the **Calvinists**, named after founder John Calvin. This group believed in the idea of predestination, or that God had already fixed each person's eternal destiny, and that only the Elect would join Him in heaven. Naturally, most people believed themselves to be among the Elect. In England, **King Henry**

VIII split from the Catholic Church after his request for an annulment from Catherine of Aragon was denied by the Pope. Henry established the **Church of England** with himself as leader, and had five more wives before his death.

> **Review Video: The Protestants**
> Visit mometrix.com/academy and enter code: 583582

COUNTER-REFORMATION

After being bombarded by Protestant attacks for years, the **Catholic Church** finally began to make some positive changes. This program was known as the **Counter-Reformation**, and it was aimed at stopping the spread of Protestantism. For instance, the sale of indulgences was halted, and more authority was given to local bishops. The Church reaffirmed many of its core teachings (such as the earning of indulgences, transubstantiation, veneration of the Virgin Mary, the necessity of works, etc.) yet admitted its errors with regard to simony and abuses of clerical power, which were quickly remedied. One of the most influential men of this movement was **Sir Ignatius Loyola**, a Spaniard who founded the **Society of Jesus (the Jesuits)** to promote the Catholic interpretation of Scripture. The **Council of Trent** was a 20-year meeting that determined the official Catholic interpretation on all matters of theology. The Counter-Reformation also saw the re-emergence of the **Inquisition**, in which heretics were sought out and punished.

> **Review Video: The Counter-Reformation**
> Visit mometrix.com/academy and enter code: 950498

INTRODUCTION OF THE ERA OF EUROPEAN MONARCHIES (1500-1650)

Between the years 1500 and 1650, most of the major European powers were led by **absolute monarchs**, who claimed a divine right to rule. These European monarchies often consolidated their power by marrying into one another. The strength of the monarchies fostered a resurgent spirit of **nationalism** and consequently led to more frequent conflicts between nations. In 1500, **Spain** was probably the most powerful nation in Europe, because of her lucrative colonies and impressive Armada. Over the next century and a half, however, **France** and **England** would emerge as the dominant powers in the region. **Germany** and **Russia**, though largely excluded from shipping, were still powerful during this period.

> **Review Video: Absolute Monarchs: An Overview**
> Visit mometrix.com/academy and enter code: 678546
>
> **Review Video: Absolute Monarchs: France**
> Visit mometrix.com/academy and enter code: 953883
>
> **Review Video: Absolute Monarchs: Germany**
> Visit mometrix.com/academy and enter code: 562601
>
> **Review Video: Absolute Monarchs: Russia**
> Visit mometrix.com/academy and enter code: 974242
>
> **Review Video: Spanish Government in the 1500s**
> Visit mometrix.com/academy and enter code: 735727

POWERS OF SPAIN BETWEEN 1500 AND 1650

The height of Spanish power began with the reign of **King Ferdinand** and **Queen Isabella**; these monarchs promoted exploration and became fantastically rich as a result. The Hapsburg **King Charles V** would increase Spain's prominence and territory, because he had acquired lands in France, Austria, and Germany through inheritance. Spain was drawn into a number of conflicts over these new possessions, however: France disputed his claim to parts of Italy, and the Ottoman Turks challenged his Armada in the Mediterranean. Charles V would finally be forced to abdicate the throne, leaving his brother **Ferdinand I** in control of Austria and Germany, and his son **Philip II** in control of Spain and some western lands. During Philip's reign, most of these possessions would be lost; particularly bitter was the loss of the Netherlands, which quickly became a trading power in their own right.

PIZARRO AND THE INCAS

Francisco Pizarro (c. 1478-1541) was a Spanish explorer. He lived for a time in what is now Panama, where he heard tales of the fabulous wealth enjoyed by the **Incas** in the Andes Mountains. **Pizarro** was determined to conquer this empire, and with 168 men he reached the Incan city of Tumbes in 1532. At this time, the Incas were in the middle of a civil war. Pizarro used this to his advantage; he massacred one side and took their leader prisoner. In order to free himself, the leader arranged a huge ransom, which Pizarro collected and then ignored, killing the leader anyway. Soon, Spaniards conquered the Incan city of **Cuzco** and installed a puppet regime. After some turmoil, Pizarro took over the leadership of **Peru** until his assassination in 1541.

CORTEZ AND HIS RELATIONSHIP WITH THE AZTECS

Hernán Cortez (1485-1547) was a Spanish conquistador. He assisted in the conquest of **Cuba** and lived there until 1518, when he was assigned to lead an expedition into **Mexico**. He and 700 men landed on the Mexican shore, and he promptly had his ships burnt in order to indicate his sincerity about establishing a foothold in the country. **Cortez** then led his troops into **Tenochtitlan**, the capital of the **Aztec Empire**. They were received graciously by the Aztec ruler, **Montezuma**, whom they immediately enslaved. The Aztecs tried to revolt against the Spanish influence, but Cortez formed a coalition with other anti-Aztec groups and brutally eliminated the Aztec uprising. Cortez went on to rule "New Spain" for a number of years.

GOVERNMENT OF FRANCE BETWEEN 1500 AND 1650

While England was undergoing a turbulent transition from an absolute to a limited monarchy, **France** was governed by a succession of powerful and talented Bourbon monarchs. The **Estates General**, the French counterpart to the British Parliament, was not especially powerful. During a period in which the Bourbon heir was too young to govern himself, the charismatic **Cardinal Richelieu** governed France. Cardinal Richelieu was a Catholic, of course, but he did not persecute the French protestant Huguenot sect. Rather, he compromised with his enemies in an attempt to consolidate the power of the French crown. Cardinal Richelieu also established a strong bureaucracy, known as the *noblesse de la robe*.

GOVERNMENT OF GERMANY BETWEEN 1500 AND 1650

Unlike many of the other Western European powers in 1500, **Germany** was still essentially just a collection of disjointed city-states. The **Hapsburg** family was powerful there, but the lands they called their **Holy Roman Empire** were not well organized, and the Hapsburgs were weak compared to other European leaders. The **Peace of Augsburg**, which had quelled disputes between Lutherans and Catholics, was destroyed by the **Thirty Years' War** (1618-48), which began when Protestants challenged the authority of the Hapsburg emperor. Germany would become so chaotic and disjointed during this period that other nations would step in, whether to seize some land or to help out one side or the other. The brutality of this war left Germany in a state of turmoil.

RUSSIAN RULE BETWEEN 1500 AND 1650

As the nations of Western Europe were beginning to rely on foreign trade almost exclusively to support themselves, **Russia** remained a feudal nation. After the Mongols were overthrown, Russia was ruled by a succession of **Czars**, and Russia was largely excluded from the cultural rejuvenation of the Renaissance period. Instead, Russians suffered through the reign of **Ivan the Terrible** (1530-84), a fierce ruler who pushed the borders out in the east with horrible brutality and suffocated any rivals or critics. Ivan's reign was so oppressive that Russia could not develop a merchant class to rival those of the Western European powers, despite having some impressive natural resources.

SCIENTIFIC REVOLUTION

The rapid advance in learning known as the **Scientific Revolution** was a product of the systematic form of inquiry known as the **scientific method**. With the scientific method, learning is incremental: a question is posed, a hypothetical solution is offered, observations are made, and the hypothesis is either supported or refuted. The consistency of the method made it easy for scientific discoveries to be transferred from one country to another. Along with a standardized form of **measurement**, the development of the scientific method gave scientists a common language. Scientists also benefited from the development of powerful **telescopes** and **microscopes**.

MAJOR FIGURES

After **Copernicus** startled the world by challenging the geocentric (that is, earth-centered) model for the universe, Italian **Galileo Galilei** supplied scientific experiments that proved the accuracy of Copernicus' theory. One of the philosophical heroes of the Scientific Revolution was Frenchman **Rene Descartes**, who attempted to base his beliefs about the world upon empirical and provable facts: most famously, "I think, therefore I am." **Francis Bacon** was an English intellectual who wrote copiously on the possibilities for science to improve the human condition. **Sir Isaac Newton** excelled in many fields but is best known for his theories of motion and gravitation. Newton helped create the general idea that objects in the world behave in regular and predictable ways.

> **Review Video: The Scientific Revolution**
> Visit mometrix.com/academy and enter code: 974600

ENGLAND DURING THE TUDOR AND STUART RULINGS

For many years, England was ruled by the **Tudor** family. **Henry VIII**, the founder of the Anglican Church, had been a Tudor, and his daughter **Elizabeth** continued his policies. During the Elizabethan age in England, trading and exploration increased, and the Spanish Armada, sent to overthrow Elizabeth as a protestant heretic, was defeated. After Elizabeth died in 1603, the **Stuart** family ascended to the throne. The Stuart period would be marked by conflict. Both **James I** and **Charles I** butted heads with Parliament over the issue of taxation, and there were also continual conflicts between **Puritans** (followers of John Calvin) and **Anglicans** (adherents of the Church of England). The Puritans joined with Parliament in opposition to the monarchy.

CROMWELL AND WILLIAM AND MARY

The alliance of Parliament and the Puritans was led by **Oliver Cromwell**. His army was successful in deposing and executing **King Charles I**, and Cromwell was subsequently installed as **Protector of England**. Cromwell's rule was undermined by Anglican nobles and clergy who disliked his Puritanism. After the death of Cromwell, England was ruled by the two sons of Charles I, **Charles II** and **James II**, the latter of which was forced to abdicate by Parliament. After this period of relative chaos, **William and Mary** of the Netherlands were asked to rule England in a limited monarchy. This shift in power was known as the **Glorious Revolution**. The **Declaration of Rights** that limited the power of the monarchy gave Parliament more power and made possible a long period of tranquility.

THE ENLIGHTENMENT

Between the years 1600 and 1770, political and social philosophy in Europe underwent a tremendous change, known collectively as the **Enlightenment**. Just as Northern Italy had been the center of the Renaissance, so now **Paris** was the hub of progressive thought. The collection of philosophers, who sought to bring every subject under the authority of reason, included both **deists** (those who believed in God) and **atheists** (those who did not). The study known as **political science** first emerged during this period. Intellectuals began to question the divine right that had been claimed by absolute monarchs in the past; they sought to determine which was the best form of government for all the citizens of the country.

> **Review Video: Age of Enlightenment**
> Visit mometrix.com/academy and enter code: 143022

MAJOR FIGURES

One of the most sparkling wits of the Enlightenment period belonged to the Frenchman **Voltaire** (1694-1778). He challenged the authority of the Church, declaring that people should tolerate the views of others and that no one man or group had a monopoly on absolute truth. **Thomas Hobbes** (1598-1679) was one of the most influential political theorists of the period. In his masterpiece "Leviathan," he declared that the base impulses of the people had to be restrained by a powerful and just monarch. **John Locke** (1632-1704), on the other hand, declared that men were born with natural rights which could not be justly denied them. **Rousseau** (1712-78), a Swiss philosopher, asserted that the government only ruled so long as it did so to the satisfaction of the general will of the people.

PEACE OF WESTPHALIA AND LOUIS XIV

The monarchs of the Enlightenment period found themselves under increasing pressure to be tolerant and benevolent. In Western Europe, so-called "enlightened despots" governed in order to promote the best interests of their subjects; this was probably done more to retain power than to express any profound solidarity with the commoners. France had become the central power on the European continent after the **Peace of Westphalia** (1648), which ended the **Thirty Years' War** and weakened Germany. The long reign of **Louis XIV** of France was characterized by grandiosity and the cultivation of the arts. Louis spent considerable effort trying to acquire new territories for France and glory for himself, and so alarmed the other European powers with his swiftness from victory to victory that many former enemies allied against France.

CREATION OF PRUSSIA AND CONTRIBUTIONS OF FREDERICK THE GREAT

The **Peace of Westphalia** (1648) established the independence of several small sections of Germany; chief among these new states was Prussia. **Frederick the Great** (1712-86) became the ruler of **Prussia** in 1740 and displayed marvelous efficiency and benevolence. He made a genuine effort to allow for the coexistence of all the religious groups in Prussia, and also worked to improve the lives of the serfs. Frederick also encouraged immigration to Prussia, which brought in new ideas and technological advances. Prussia, which had long suffered economically because of its lack of a coastline, now became a producer of luxury goods like porcelain and silk.

Russia During the Rule of Peter the Great and Catherine the Great

Peter the Great (1672-1725) was responsible for the transformation of Russia from an impoverished agricultural nation to a strong commercial nation. Peter was enamored of the ways of the western European nations and made several trips to other capitals to learn the intricacies of Enlightenment politics and trade. **St. Petersburg** was intended to be a Russian city in the style of Paris or Berlin. Peter's innovations revitalized the economy, but they also set a standard for decadence that would be carried on by future czars. **Catherine II**, otherwise known as Catherine the Great, ruled from 1762 to 1796 and implemented many Enlightenment policies in education and the arts. Nevertheless, in the remote provinces of Russia, the **feudal system** endured, and the economy remained stunted.

French Revolution

Causes

Before the revolution, France was governed by an absolute monarch and, with regard to matters of taxation, the **Estates General**, which had been formed in order to represent the common people. The Estates General was composed of three estates: the clergy (**First Estate**), nobility (**Second Estate**), and everyone else (**Third Estate**). Unfortunately, this body had been marginalized by a series of powerful monarchs, and it was arranged such that the largest group by far, the Third Estate, only had one-third of the vote. In any case, the Third Estate usually found its desires opposed by the other estates. Another source of anger for the middle class and peasants was the **tax structure**; the nobles and clergy were not forced to pay taxes, and thus the burden of France's depressed economy fell upon the Third Estate.

King Louis XVI and National Assembly

Aware of the injustice of the French tax policy, **King Louis XVI** tried to pass some reforms but was repeatedly thwarted by the greedy nobles and clergy. The **Third Estate** was infuriated and refused to vote in the Estates General anymore. Instead, prominent members of the middle class banded together to form the **National Assembly**, which purported to represent the interests of common Frenchmen. At the same time, the peasants were in full revolt. On July 14, 1789, they stormed the Parisian prison known as the **Bastille**. The success of this riot inspired more peasants to clamor for representation, and the diversion it caused kept the government from dealing with the National Assembly.

Declaration of the Rights of Man

After the storming of the Bastille and the formation of the National Assembly in 1789, the French middle and lower classes joined together and established a new government with the slogan "**Liberty, Equality, Fraternity**." This government quickly reformed the tax code and declared that government offices would henceforth be filled on the basis of merit. The National Assembly also eliminated serfdom and drafted a **Declaration of the Rights of Man**, which was similar to the American Bill of Rights. The National Assembly then seized the lands that belonged to the Church and eliminated the feudal rights of the aristocracy. Soon, there was dissension within the Third Estate, and the revolution became more radical and violent.

French Revolution and the Reign of Terror

As the government established by the Third Estate descended into chaos, the radical Jacobin leader **Robespierre** took charge. He had an idealistic vision of what France could become, and he was willing to kill thousands in order to see it realized. The **guillotine** provided a swift way to execute scores of opponents, a group that included anyone who dared challenge the Jacobin party line or was suspected of retaining their Catholic faith in the new culture of state-mandated atheism.

Among those executed were **King Louis XVI** and his wife, **Marie Antoinette**. After a while, the French tired of the violence and turmoil of the **Reign of Terror**, and Robespierre himself fell victim to the guillotine. A group of five prominent men, known as the **Directory**, was established to restore calm. This group would last until 1799, when it was overthrown in a coup that would eventually bring **Napoleon Bonaparte** to power.

RISE OF NAPOLEON BONAPARTE

Napoleon Bonaparte (1769-1821) began his career as a French military commander, scoring major victories in Austria and England. Upon his return to the chaos of France, he led a coup and was installed as the leader of France. He was subsequently elected by a popular vote. Almost immediately, **Napoleon** reformed French education, agriculture, and infrastructure. The main object of Napoleon's rule, however, was the acquisition of territory both in Europe and in the New World. Napoleon's troops quickly conquered Austria, Portugal, Spain, and Prussia. Napoleon, who modeled himself after Charlemagne in many ways, then crowned himself **emperor**. The French empire proved too large to manage, however, and Napoleon further weakened himself with a disastrous campaign against Russia.

> **Review Video: The French Revolution: Napoleon Bonaparte**
> Visit mometrix.com/academy and enter code: 876330

INDEPENDENCE STRUGGLE IN LATIN AMERICA

When Spain fell to Napoleon's forces in 1809, the provinces of **Chile** and **Buenos Aires** both declared themselves independent. At this time, **Peru** was the stronghold of Spanish power in the New World, and therefore the rebels attacked the government there. Led by the Argentinean **Jose San Martin**, rebels entered Lima and declared Peru an independent state in 1821. The greatest military leader of the independence movement, however, was **Simon Bolivar**. He had traveled extensively in Europe and used his knowledge of the enemy to run the Spaniards out of Colombia, Venezuela, and Central America. Bolivar eventually seized control of Peru and hoped to form a great union of South American nations, but this alliance was eventually torn asunder by internal feuds.

FALL OF NAPOLEON

After Napoleon's debacle in Russia debilitated his military, revolts sprung up in many of the nations that he had conquered, and Napoleon was overthrown. The leaders of the countries that had overthrown Napoleon met in Vienna to decide how to respond to him. These three men, **Prince von Metternich** of Austria, the English **Duke of Wellington**, and **Alexander I** of Russia, were constantly in disagreement, however, and Napoleon used this opportunity to return from his exile on the Isle of Elba in the Mediterranean and reclaim power. Finally, Napoleon was defeated at **Waterloo** and sent into permanent exile. The allies met again at the **Congress of Vienna** in 1815 where France was not treated too harshly, and it was determined that a balance of power should be maintained in Europe to ensure that no one in the future tried to dominate the continent.

OPIUM WAR

The Opium War lasted between the years 1839 and 1842. It began because the British kept trafficking **opium** from India into China because they wanted to trade with the Chinese, and opium was the only product that China could not produce for itself. The Chinese government, however, was appalled by the effect that the drug had on its citizens and mounted a serious anti-opium campaign. When British merchants appealed to their leaders, the British navy was sent in order to force the Chinese to accept the opium. The British ended up seizing several Chinese cities, including

Shanghai and Nanking. The war ended with the **Treaty of Nanking** in 1842; China was forced to cede Hong Kong to the British, and several Chinese ports had to be left open for trade.

> **Review Video: Anti-Colonial Struggles: The Opium War**
> Visit mometrix.com/academy and enter code: 111806

TAIPING REBELLION

The Taiping Rebellion lasted in China between the years 1850 and 1864. It was a religious and political rebellion against the government of the **Manchus**, led by the Christian **Hung Hsiu-ch'uan**. The rebels advocated the public ownership of land and a self-sufficient economy. They wanted to rid China of the encroaching influences of foreign merchants. Hung's troops were able to conquer Nanking and make it the capital of their "Great Peaceful Heavenly Dynasty." Internal feuds weakened the Taiping, however, and the western powers (concerned that they would lose the Chinese market) helped to oust them in 1864. The **Taiping Rebellion** was by far the bloodiest war of the 19th century.

MEIJI REFORM

In 1854, an American group led by **Commodore Matthew Perry** forced Japan to open its ports to foreign merchants. Japan had been closed to the West for 200 years. The Japanese people were not pleased with this development, and they blamed the **Tokugawa shogun** (the military leader of the period). In 1867, the shogun resigned and **Emperor Matsuhito** declared that he was now in charge. The Japanese capital was moved from Kyoto to Edo (which was renamed Tokyo). The ensuing period in Japanese history is known as the **Meiji Period**. During it, the feudal system was abolished, and Western ideas became popular. The samurai had their land right revoked and were eventually eliminated altogether. In the late 19th century, Japanese leaders began to turn their attentions to expansion onto the Asian continent; in the Sino-Japanese war, they conquered parts of China and Korea.

BOXER REBELLION

The Boxer Rebellion was a peasant uprising in China around the turn of the 20th century. The rebels aimed to overthrow the **Manchu government** and to cast all foreigners out of China. The rebels were known as the **Boxers** because they practiced certain mystical boxing rituals. After Japan had defeated China in 1895, the Japanese had exercised a great deal of influence on the Chinese economy. Around 1900, Boxers began to kill foreign merchants and diplomats. An international force was assembled to defeat the Boxers. During the ensuing fight, the city of **Peking** was almost entirely destroyed. Eventually, the western powers prevailed and forced the Boxer leaders to sign an incredibly unfavorable treaty.

> **Review Video: Anti-Colonial Struggles: The Boxer Rebellion**
> Visit mometrix.com/academy and enter code: 352161

INDUSTRIAL REVOLUTION

ENGLISH TEXTILE INDUSTRY

The **Industrial Revolution** in Europe in the 19th century produced immediate and far-reaching changes in the social structure. **England** was perhaps the first to feel the effects of rapid industrialization; the factory system for manufacturing textiles was implemented, meaning that individuals were only required to do one in the series of tasks required to prepare a piece of cloth. This division of labor increased productivity. New energy sources, such as the steam engine, also made fabulous increases in productivity possible. Coal was introduced as an aid to the iron-smelting process, and the mass production of cotton textiles was soon propelling the English economy.

SOCIAL CHANGES

With the success of the textile industry, more and more workers were needed in the European cities, and therefore people began to abandon their country lives and take factory jobs in town. This rapid **urbanization** created a new **middle class** in Europe, and it also created a number of problems. Most cities did not have the infrastructure to support such an explosion in population, and as such, disease, crime, and poverty were common. The booming success of industry made many people rich as investors and merchants, and therefore the middle class assumed even more political power in Europe. **Social mobility** was infinitely more possible in this economic environment, encouraging many people to stick with jobs that were demeaning and not especially lucrative.

WORKING CLASS AND LUDDITES

As people flooded the cities to work in the booming factories, large landowners consolidated the farmlands they left behind. **Working-class** individuals were probably not pleased with their new lives; 18-hour days, low wages, and dangerous machinery were among the problems faced by this new underclass. Oftentimes, women and children were employed for the most menial jobs, and they were paid less than men. A small rebellion, led by a group called the **Luddites**, tried to resist the tide of industrialization and were known for vandalizing factory equipment. Still, most individuals were enticed by the prospect of upward mobility that the new, fluid class system offered, and were willing to endure hardship in exchange for hope.

> **Review Video: The Industrial Revolution**
> Visit mometrix.com/academy and enter code: 372796
>
> **Review Video: Industrialization**
> Visit mometrix.com/academy and enter code: 893924

NATIONALISM IN 19TH-CENTURY EUROPE

In the 19th century, the spirit of nationalism that had been building in Europe since the Middle Ages reached a critical mass. **Nationalism** refers to pride in the traditions, culture, language, and past of a certain nation of people, and not necessarily to pride in one's country. This is important to note, because in the 19th century, there were many nations of people thrown together as parts of a larger kingdom. The rising tide of nationalism, then, was a concern to the ruling **monarchs**, who hoped to hold together disparate nations under their control. Russia, for instance, contained a wide variety of cultures and languages under one leadership.

> **Review Video: Historical Nationalism**
> Visit mometrix.com/academy and enter code: 510185

CLASSICAL LIBERALISM IN 19TH-CENTURY EUROPE

The political and economic philosophies of the Enlightenment laid the foundation for 19th-century **classical liberalism**. **Adam Smith's** "The Wealth of Nations," written in 1776, introduced the concept of the "invisible hand," suggesting that market forces, if left largely to operate freely, could lead to economic prosperity. Although Smith's work preceded the Industrial Revolution, his ideas influenced later classical liberals who championed free-market policies. Another influential thinker, **Thomas Malthus**, in "An Essay on the Principle of Population" (1798), wrote that unchecked population growth would outstrip food supply, leading to famine and disease. While his work was later used to justify laissez-faire economic policies, Malthus himself advocated for population control measures rather than the outright suffering of the poor.

SOCIAL LIBERALISM IN 19TH-CENTURY EUROPE

Social liberalism developed in the late 19th century as an alternative to classical liberalism. **Social liberalism** declares that political problems can be solved by the work of liberal institutions in the government. Unlike the classical liberals, social liberals believe that the government should exercise some influence on the **economy** and should extend some basic **welfare services** to the people. Social liberalism aimed to improve life for the poor and disadvantaged. Social liberals were also very outspoken on issues of civil rights and individual liberties. Some of the most famous social liberals are **Jeremy Bentham**, **John Stuart Mill**, and **John Dewey**.

EMERGENCE OF SOCIALISM IN 19TH-CENTURY EUROPE

Socialism is a political philosophy which declares that the economic means of production should be owned by the workers. This control may either be exercised directly by the workers through local councils or by the state with the consent of the workers. Socialists hope thereby to create a state of **social equality** and an even **distribution of wealth**. Not surprisingly, this movement was most popular among the working classes in 19th-century Europe. Socialists at this time declared that capitalism served only the interests of the very wealthy and exploited everyone else. In their view, a socialist society would provide a greater reward for hard work and would create harmonious societies. Socialism and communism come from the same ideological lineage, but they differ in some ways. Generally speaking, socialism and communism both hope to have the means of production controlled by a collective or governing organization and not owned privately. **Socialism** would allow for individuals to continue to have private property, whereas **communism** would eliminate private property and have the collective or state regulate the distribution of wealth.

> **Review Video: Communism vs. Socialism**
> Visit mometrix.com/academy and enter code: 917677

EMERGENCE OF MARXISM IN 19TH-CENTURY EUROPE

The political theories of socialism and communism both take their inspiration from the works of **Karl Marx** (1818-83). Marx declared that economics has been the primary determinant in history and that the history of society is nothing more than a "history of class struggle." Marx asserted that problems have been created in situations where the material that a worker produces is worth more than the compensation he receives for his work. The surplus goes to the capitalist owner, and the worker is caught in a situation where he can never get ahead. The inevitable result, according to Marx, is a revolution of the working class (which he called the **proletariat**) and the installation of an economic system similar to socialism or communism.

> **Review Video: Karl Marx**
> Visit mometrix.com/academy and enter code: 362061

19TH-CENTURY BRITISH POLITICS

During the 19th century, the memory of Napoleon and the balance of power established by the **Congress of Vienna** prevented any large conflicts. The **Industrial Revolution** had made Britain the wealthiest and most powerful nation in Europe. The rise of a rich middle class caused the British Parliament to alter voting laws so that more of the wealthy would have influence. This was done with the **Reform Act of 1832**; in 1833, Britain abolished slavery in its colonies. This was not enough for the many working-class Britons, however, and they lobbied long and hard for universal suffrage until it was finally granted in the 1880s. The British movement for universal suffrage was known as **Chartism**.

> **Review Video: 19th Century Politics: Britain**
> Visit mometrix.com/academy and enter code: 266214

19TH-CENTURY FRENCH POLITICS

Internal turmoil caused France to miss out on much of the wealth of the Industrial Revolution. After the demise of Napoleon, **Louis XVII** had been restored to the throne by the **Congress of Vienna**. He was succeeded by the archconservative **Charles X**, who was quite unpopular and was chased off the throne in the **July Revolution of 1830**. In his place came **Louis Philippe**, who administered over a fairly stable country for eighteen years until he was deposed in the revolution of 1848. Next came **Napoleon III**. Elected the emperor of France in 1851, he remained in power until the French defeat in the **Franco-Prussian War of 1870**. From 1870 until 1940, France would be governed by a constitutional and democratic government that was, for the most part, conservative.

19TH-CENTURY GERMAN POLITICAL SYSTEM

Ever since the end of Charlemagne's empire, Austria and Germany had not been unified as a single nation. This was finally achieved by the Prussian **Otto von Bismarck** after a long period of suppression of German nationalists. Bismarck's unification of **Prussia** was mainly aimed at defeating the rival Hapsburgs, who controlled Austria. When Prussia won the **Austro-Prussian** and **Franco-Prussian wars** in quick succession, Bismarck declared that he had achieved his ends and unified the German empire. He oversaw the creation of the **Reichstag**, a legislative body that would provide representation to the middle and lower classes. Germany threw itself into the project of industrialization.

19TH-CENTURY ITALIAN POLITICAL SYSTEM

Italy, like Germany, had really been more of a disjointed collection of independent city-states than a nation in its own right. In the 19th century, however, there was a drive to unify the region. A leader from the Piedmont region, **Camillo Cavour**, tried to bring the various city-states together through diplomacy rather than combat. This process took a very long time but was eventually completed in the 1870s. **Northern Italy**, which had intimate contact with Germany, became industrialized during this period, and the city of Milan enjoyed immense growth. **Southern Italy**, on the other hand, remained largely rural. This distinction between the two halves of Italy would be a source of conflict in the future.

19TH-CENTURY RUSSIAN POLITICAL SYSTEM

At the beginning of the 19th century, much of Russia was still mired in an impoverished, quasi-feudal state. After the death of **Alexander** in 1825, the **Decembrists** tried to force the incoming Czar to adopt a constitution allocating some power to the people. The next czar was **Nicholas I**, who used secret police to try to eliminate the roots of the popular insurrection. This policy of suppression only further isolated Russia from the rest of Europe, which was at that time reducing the power of the monarch. Russia later lost the **Crimean War** to Britain, France, and the Ottoman Empire, and many Russians bemoaned the backward state of their country. Finally, a new czar, **Alexander II**, freed the serfs and tried to industrialize. This happened slowly.

RUSSIAN REVOLUTION OF 1905

At the turn of the 20th century, **Russia** was torn by the trends of industrialism and imperialism. The country was still being operated as an absolute monarchy, and was behind on social reforms common to the rest of Europe. Russia was trying to undergo rapid industrial expansion in the cities.

Russia experienced a humiliating defeat of their navy in the **Russo-Japanese War,** causing increased labor unrest and dissatisfaction with the strong monarchy. The socialist party in Russia split into the **Bolsheviks,** who favored immediate socialist reform, and the **Mensheviks,** who favored gradual reforms and cooperation. When a peaceful demonstration against the czar was brutally suppressed, rebel forces made up of political activists, peasants, and workers became energized, leading to the **Russian Revolution of 1905.** This revolution continued with revolts by peasants and soldiers, until the czar promised to create a constitutional monarchy with a powerful legislative body, known as the **Duma**. These changes promised civil liberties and a parliamentary process, but the Tsar soon after went back on his word and limited the power of the Duma, leading to increased civil unrest.

Chapter Quiz

Ready to see how well you retained what you just read? Scan the QR code to go directly to the chapter quiz interface for this study guide. If you're using a computer, simply visit the online resources page at mometrix.com/resources719/apworldhistory-27797 and click the Chapter Quizzes link.

World History: 1914 to Present

Transform passive reading into active learning! After immersing yourself in this chapter, put your comprehension to the test by taking a quiz. The insights you gained will stay with you longer this way. Scan the QR code to go directly to the chapter quiz interface for this study guide. If you're using a computer, simply visit the online resources page at **mometrix.com/resources719/apworldhistory-27797** and click the Chapter Quizzes link.

ENTANGLING ALLIANCES PRIOR TO WWI

In the early years of the 20th century, relations among the various European powers were complex. Ever since the **Franco-Prussian War**, won by Prussia, the two sides had been enemies. At the center of their conflict was the territory of **Alsace-Lorraine**, which each side claimed as its own. In order to bolster their position in the region, each side entered into networks of alliances. After years of negotiations, two main alliances contained the major European powers: the **Triple Alliance** (Germany, Austria, Italy) and the **Triple Entente** (France, Britain, Russia). These two alliances would end up being the opposing sides in the great war of the ensuing years.

THE BALKANS AND BEGINNING OF WWI

In the years before the First World War, the **Balkans** were attempting to gain independence from the Hapsburg empire of Austria. This insurrection culminated in the assassination of Austrian **Archduke Franz Ferdinand** in 1914 by **Gavrilo Princip**, a member of a Serbian nationalist group. At this point, a chain reaction of war declarations (spurred by the comprehensive alliances of the time) ensued. Austria declared war against Serbia, Germany and Turkey joined with the Austrians, Russia declared war on these countries in support of Serbia, France joined with Russia, and Britain and Italy joined forces with France, even though Italy had been a member of the Triple Alliance.

COMBAT AND EXIT OF RUSSIA DURING WWI

Despite the fact that almost every nation in Europe had entered into World War I, most Europeans thought the conflict would be brief. Instead, advances in **weapons technology** made the war bloody and excruciatingly slow. Much of the fighting was done from **trenches**, and some battles would see the deaths of thousands of soldiers at a time. The war was also slow because the sides were very evenly matched; that is, until 1917, when the United States entered on the side of Britain. Also, in 1917, the Russians exited the war via the **Brest-Litovsk Treaty**. Russia was basically exhausted after suffering through a Revolution in 1917 in which the **Bolsheviks** came to power. The entry of the US provided the British and French with supplies and troops, and Germany was soon forced to call for a truce.

TREATY OF VERSAILLES

As the First World War wound down, a disgruntled German populace ousted the emperor and installed a moderate socialist government. This government, known as the **Weimar Republic**, would last until 1933. At the **Paris Peace Conference**, the victors of the war (the US, Britain, France, and Italy) exacted some revenge on Germany. The **Treaty of Versailles** penalized Germany economically and territorially; Alsace-Lorraine became independent, and the German military was dismantled. The Treaty of Versailles would need to be modified by two subsequent agreements: the **Treaty of Locarno,** which outlined a more reasonable reparations plan for Germany, and the

Kellogg-Briand Pact, which asserted that diplomacy rather than force would be used to resolve conflicts.

WESTERN EUROPE AND ITALY AFTER THE FIRST WORLD WAR

In the years after the First World War, the general mood in Europe was one of wariness. Most nations were exhausted by the conflict, and few felt that the signing of the **Treaty of Versailles** and the formation of the **League of Nations** had created a permanent peace. In the 1920s, Britain, Germany, France, and the United States were all liberal democracies without a strong executive. Unlike the United States, however, the European nations suffered a profound economic depression. One nation that saw no diminution in nationalism was **Italy**. In part out of a fear of communism, Italians supported the rise of the fascist dictator **Benito Mussolini**. **Fascism** is defined as an extreme-right movement characterized by totalitarian rule with an emphasis on national unity and identity. Fascism generally manifests in dictatorial rule and suppression of the free speech and rights of dissenters. It originated in Italy and promised to the Italians a return to the glory days of Rome, when they were a mighty power ruled by a dominating executive. Of course, in order to maintain his authority, Mussolini had to brutally suppress any opposition.

RUSSIAN REVOLUTION OF 1917

After the **Revolution of 1905**, Russia had enjoyed a few years of relative peace. After a while, however, the peasants became dissatisfied with the weakness of the Duma, and after strikes and protests, **Czar Nicholas II** was forced to abdicate the throne. In place of the monarchy, a **provisional government** was set up to work alongside more progressive local councils, known as **Soviets**. These two groups were constantly at odds, however, especially during Russia's participation in the **First World War** (the Soviets wanted to withdraw and focus on national issues, while the Provisional Government felt obliged to fight). During this period, **Vladimir Lenin** rose to prominence as the Marxist leader of the **Bolshevik Party**. In the **Russian Revolution of 1917**, Lenin and his supporters ousted the provisional government and exited the war. Lenin then began the immense project of nationalizing the Soviet economy.

LENIN AND STALIN

After his success in the Revolution of 1917, **Lenin** began to advocate the revolt of the working class in other nations. Naturally, this did not endear the new Russian government to the leaders of other nations. Russia became increasingly isolated both economically and politically from the rest of the world. Domestically, Lenin established the **New Economic Policy**, which blended capitalism and communism. This plan worked well enough in agriculture, but it never achieved much success in industry. After Lenin's death, **Joseph Stalin** came to power and began an ambitious plan of collectivizing farms and nationalizing factories (known as the **Five Year Plans**). Stalin was ruthless in the pursuit of his goals; he established labor camps to house his opponents. It is estimated that 20 million people were killed by Stalin's regime during the period now known as the **Great Terror**.

CHINA IN THE EARLY 20H CENTURY

In 1911, the **Manchu dynasty**, which had been significantly weakened by the **Boxer Rebellion**, was finally overthrown. A period of instability followed, in which **Sun Yat-sen** declared the creation of a republic with its headquarters in Nanking. Sun Yat-sen began a political party aimed at improving life for the common people; it was known as the **Kuomintang**. During this period, both Mongolia and Tibet declared their independence from China. The Chinese people became disenchanted with the Kuomintang government after what they saw as unfavorable agreements following World War I. After the death of Sun Yat-sen in 1925, a national government was established at Canton; the **communist party** was a major participant in this government.

Rule of the Kuomintang and the Sino-Japanese War in 20th-Century China

In 1926, the military leader **Chiang Kai-shek** led campaigns in central and northern China, in the hopes of unifying the country. During this period, Chiang broke with the **communist party**, and Communists were persecuted in Shanghai. In 1927, a national government led by the **Kuomintang**, who had previously fallen out of favor, was established in Nanking. The peasants were not pleased with this leadership, and they were organized as the **Red Army** under **Mao Tse-tung** in the south. In what is known as the **Long March**, Mao led his army north to Yenan, where they would gather strength. The situation in China was made even more volatile by the Japanese invasion in 1937. In what is known as the "**Rape of Nanking**," Japanese troops killed over 200,000 Chinese. The people were outraged, and the partisan splits between Mao's communists and Chiang's government only widened.

Japan in the Years Before WWII

In 1926, amid growing nationalism, **Hirohito** became the Emperor of Japan. The next year, the Japanese prime minister declared that Japan should dominate Asia, and four years later, Japanese forces invaded **Manchuria**. Some historians consider this to be the beginning of the Second World War. After establishing a puppet regime in Manchuria, the Japanese withdrew from the League of Nations and attacked China. The **Sino-Japanese War** ensued. In 1938, Japan outlined its new vision of **Co-Prosperity Spheres**; Japan would be the industrial center of Asia and would acquire its raw materials from its colonies in the rest of Asia. Japan promoted this idea as an opportunity to break from European imperialism, but it was really just the substitution of one master for another. In 1940, Japan would complete its transformation into a **fascist state** by dissolving all political parties.

Events Leading to World War II in Europe

Still shell-shocked from the First World War, the nations of western Europe were slow to respond to the growing menace of **Nazi Germany**. In general, they pursued a policy of appeasement and isolation. The British prime minister **Neville Chamberlain** was especially committed to using diplomacy over war. Then, in 1936, Hitler sent troops to occupy the **Rhineland**, a strip of territory on the German border. At around the same time, **Mussolini** invaded Ethiopia; the two aggressors, Germany and Italy, entered into an agreement making them the **Axis Powers**. In 1938, Germany annexed Austria and indicated that it was about to attack Czechoslovakia. In response to these actions, Chamberlain brought together Mussolini and Hitler for the **Munich Conference of 1938**. These talks would only briefly suspend German aggression.

Weimar Republic and the Rise of Hitler

After the abdication of the emperor, Germany was ruled by a legislative body known as the **Weimar Republic**. Most Germans felt that this group had been too willing to accept punishment in the treaties that followed the war. Germans also thought that this government was responsible for the **inflation** which crippled the German economy in the post-war period. Germany, then, was vulnerable to the charms of a leader who told them they had nothing about which to be ashamed. This leader was **Adolf Hitler** (1889-1945). A failed artist, Hitler became the head of the **National Socialist**, or **Nazi**, party. His speeches were expressions of ardent nationalism, although often Hitler seemed to be calling for a return to an ideal German state that had never actually existed.

Belief System of the Nazi Party

Led by **Adolf Hitler**, the Nazi party championed the **Aryan race** as superior to all others, especially the "insidious" Jews. Hitler suggested that the noble ambitions of the true German people required *lebensraum*, or living space. In other words, Germany needed more territory. In its early days, the Nazi party was part of the German republican system; Nazi candidates ran for office and served in the **Reichstag** (German parliament). As Germany suffered through a terrible economic depression in the early 1930s, however, the people became impatient. In 1933, the Reichstag "accidentally" caught on fire, and the Nazis used the opportunity to claim total control of the government. Hitler was named **Chancellor of Germany**. He was able to quickly improve the German economy, mostly through the expansion of the weapon-building industry. At the same time, the new government began to quietly round up Jews, Gypsies, and homosexuals.

HOLOCAUST

As **Germany** sank deeper and deeper into dire economic straits, the tendency was to look for a person or group of people to blame for the problems of the country. With distrust of the **Jewish people** already ingrained, it was easy for German authorities to set up the Jews as scapegoats for Germany's problems.

The Holocaust is the name given to the systematic killing of Jews, Gypsies, homosexuals, and others by the Nazis. **Anti-Semitism** had existed in Europe for millennia, but the Nazis gave it renewed emphasis and, after making numerous false claims about Jews, began persecuting them upon Hitler's rise to power in 1933. Jews were disenfranchised, forced into ghettos, had their property taken, and were finally sent to work and be killed in **concentration camps**. Approximately 6 million Jews were killed during the **Holocaust**. As the situation for the Germans became more dire in the Second World War, Hitler sought to implement what he called the "final solution," in which hundreds of thousands were killed just before the fall of Nazi Germany.

The Allies were aware of rumors of mass slaughter throughout the war, but many discounted the reports. Only when troops went in to liberate the prisoners was the true horror of the concentration camps brought to light.

> **Review Video: The Holocaust**
> Visit mometrix.com/academy and enter code: 350695

CONSEQUENCES OF THE HOLOCAUST

Many of the Nazi leaders were tried and convicted at the **Nuremberg trials** for their roles in the Holocaust. West Germany would later issue a **Federal Compensation Law**, through which billions of dollars were paid to survivors. During and after the Holocaust, Zionist Jews fled to **Palestine**. Public sympathy with their plight would be one of the main reasons for the creation of **Israel** in 1948. The total destruction of the Jewish community in Europe caused many Jews to question their faith, and those that remained in Europe are markedly more secular than their ancestors. The shock of the Holocaust has also caused many institutions, including the Roman Catholic Church, to consider their own latent anti-Semitism. Unfortunately, the anti-genocide legislation created in response to the Holocaust was not strict enough to rally international support against the **Rwandans** (who slaughtered hundreds of thousands of Tutsis in 1994) or the **Bosnian Serbs and Croats** (who killed thousands of Muslims in the early 1990s).

PACIFIC ARENA IN WWII

The **Japanese**, like the Germans, became seduced by the notion of their own racial superiority during the 1930s. As in Germany, this inevitably led to a lust for territorial expansion. By 1941, Japan had conquered Korea, Manchuria, and parts of China. Japan was also threatening to invade American interests in the Philippines. The United States imposed **economic sanctions** on Japan, making it difficult for the Japanese war industry to function. In response, the Japanese launched a surprise attack on the United States by bombing the US naval base of **Pearl Harbor**. After the attack on Pearl Harbor, the United States declared war upon Japan (and Germany, in turn, declared war on the United States). The Japanese made huge territorial gains before the US turned the tide at the **Battles of Midway and Guadalcanal**. The war in the Pacific would take much longer than the war in Europe due to the island-hopping nature of the fight. The unwillingness of the Japanese to surrender made it almost impossible for America to entirely vanquish them without enormous loss of life. So, the United States decided to drop atomic bombs on **Hiroshima** and **Nagasaki** to force Japan to surrender and finally end the war in the Pacific in August 1945.

BEGINNING AND INITIAL YEARS OF WORLD WAR II IN EUROPE

After **Chamberlain** had tried to forestall German aggression at the **Munich Conference of 1938**, Germany nevertheless invaded Czechoslovakia in 1939. It was also during this year that Hitler signed a secret agreement with **Stalin** pledging not to attack Russia so long as Russia stayed out of German affairs. Hitler then declared war on and conquered Poland. At this step, Great Britain and France were finally forced to declare war upon Germany. Germany at this point was a dominating military adversary. New advances in motorized military vehicles made it possible for Germany to conquer large areas of land quickly in a new form of warfare called **Blitzkrieg** (lightning war). The **Axis powers** conquered almost the entire European continent, including France, over the course of 1940. Only Great Britain remained in opposition, and the Nazis undertook a ferocious aerial assault on the British, who were by then led by **Winston Churchill**, but failed to do enough damage to make an invasion of the island country practical. Instead, Hitler turned east and decided to violate his truce with Stalin, invading **Russia** in 1941. The Germans overwhelmed much of the Soviet military and advanced deep into Russian territory in a huge surprise offensive.

MIDDLE YEARS AND CONCLUSION OF WORLD WAR II IN EUROPE

The tide turned against Hitler once the United States entered the war. The harsh Russian winter halted the German advance into Russia short of Moscow in 1941. The Germans made further gains in the summer of 1942 but were decisively beaten at the **Battle of Stalingrad** and were slowly pushed back out of Russia from then on. American and British troops landed in North Africa in 1942 and used that as a springboard to invade Italy in 1943. In 1944, the Americans and British opened yet another front with a massive invasion of northern France in the **D-Day landings**. Fighting numerically superior forces on multiple fronts, the Germans steadily lost ground and the Allies pushed into Germany from both East and West in 1945. Surrounded and with the war lost, Hitler committed **suicide** in his bunker in Berlin in April 1945, and the remaining German forces **surrendered** shortly afterward.

INDIA AND PAKISTAN AFTER WWII

In 1947, after years of peaceful protests led by **Mahatma Gandhi**, India was given its independence and partitioned into two states, **India** and **Pakistan**. The following year, Gandhi would be assassinated in India. In 1965, border disputes would flare into the **Indo-Pakistani War**. In 1971, Pakistan would fend off attacks from Bengali rebels, who sought to achieve independence. The next year, however, **Bangladesh** would be established as an independent state. In 1984, India had its own internal problems; after the Indian army occupied the **Golden Temple** sacred to the Sikhs, the Indian leader **Indira Gandhi** was assassinated by her Sikh bodyguards. **Anti-Sikh riots** resulted, and much blood was shed.

BEGINNINGS OF THE COLD WAR

After the defeat of the Axis powers in WWII, the United States and Russia entered into a long and often secret conflict, in which each side used diplomatic, economic, and occasionally military forces to try to assert itself as the dominant world power. The first issue on which these nations butted heads was the **rebuilding of Europe**. Germany was divided into an eastern and western section; the western half was democratic and looked to the US for guidance, while Eastern Germany became a communist nation in the USSR's sphere of influence. Russia worked to bring all of its neighbors (including Poland, Czechoslovakia, Hungary, Romania, and Bulgaria) under its control. The western borders of these nations formed what Churchill referred to as the **iron curtain**, dividing communist Eastern Europe from democratic Western Europe.

Truman Doctrine, Marshall Plan, NATO, and Warsaw Pact

In order to stop the spread of communism in Europe and elsewhere, President Truman asserted his policy of "containment" in the so-called **Truman Doctrine**. This meant that the US would support the anticommunist governments throughout the world. The **Marshall Plan** advanced this policy by supplying aid to war-ravaged countries in Western Europe. When the **Eastern Bloc countries** prevented aid from reaching West Berlin, the US, England, and France organized the **Berlin Airlift** to overcome this obstacle. In 1949, the Western European and North American nations entered into a mutual defense treaty, NATO (North Atlantic Treaty Organization). As a response, the Eastern Bloc nations joined with the Soviet Union in the **Warsaw Pact**.

Communist Revolution in China

China was torn by civil strife all throughout the Second World War. At one point, the American government had to renounce its trade rights in **China** in order to persuade China not to sign a peace treaty with Japan while the US still needed Chinese support. Once Japan had been defeated, the **Red Army** under Mao moved into **Manchuria** (which had recently been vacated by the Soviets). The major cities were still occupied by Nationalist forces, supported by the Americans. In 1946, fighting resumed between the opposing factions, and the **Nationalists** under Chiang were eventually forced to abandon central China. In 1949, the Red Army forced Chiang Kai-shek to leave the mainland and find refuge in Taiwan. On October 1, 1949, the communists declared the official creation of the **People's Republic of China**.

Arms Race, Cuban Missile Crisis, and Bay of Pigs in the Cold War

During the **Cold War**, the United States and the Soviet Union each tried to deter an attack by the other by building up fantastic arsenals of **nuclear missiles**. The two nations would also expend considerable effort trying to be the first in space. Finally, in the late 60s and early 70s, the two nations would begin talks aimed at mutual disarmament. This occurred in part because relations between China and the USSR had cooled. Before this period of détente, however, there had been a couple of serious threats to global peace. In 1961, the US had financed an unsuccessful invasion of Cuba at the **Bay of Pigs**. This led the Soviet Union to establish missile bases on communist Cuba; the US and USSR almost declared war on one another during the **Cuban Missile Crisis of 1962**.

End of the Cold War

Over time, the leaders of the Soviet Union and United States began to realize the total annihilation that would ensue if nuclear war was declared, and it was agreed that both sides would **disarm**. The two treaties that were signed during the 1970s are known as the **Strategic Arms Limitation Talks (SALT) I and II**. When **Mikhail Gorbachev** came into power in the USSR in 1985, he established a policy of **glasnost**, or "openness." In response to US President Ronald Reagan's military build-up using the might of the US economy, Gorbachev understood that the Soviet Union could not economically compete militarily under a communist system and overcome the military might of the United States. He thus advocated **perestroika**, a gradual metamorphosis of the Soviet economy. In 1991, these reforms culminated in the disintegration of the ruling Communist party, and the

disbanding of the Soviet Union. This occurred two years after the **Berlin Wall**, which for more than forty years had separated communist and anticommunist Germany, was finally torn down.

> **Review Video: The End of the Cold War**
> Visit mometrix.com/academy and enter code: 278032

MIDDLE EAST FROM 1947 TO 1977

After WWII, the United Nations announced that **Palestine** would be partitioned in order to make room for a new Jewish state. **Israel** was created in 1948. In 1951, the Iranian leader **Mossadegh** nationalized the oil interests, making his government extremely wealthy and powerful. This move would be emulated by future leaders. In 1967, in the **Six-Day War**, Israel routed a coalition of Arab nations, seizing the West Bank, Sinai, and Jerusalem. In 1972, Palestinian terrorists murdered 12 Israeli athletes at the Olympics in Munich. In 1973, the oil-producing Arab nations placed an embargo on shipments to the West, causing major energy crises in the US and Europe. Also, in 1973, Israelis and Arabs battled again in the **Yom Kippur War**. In 1977, Egyptian leader **Anwar Sadat** became the first Arab leader to visit Israel.

MIDDLE EAST FROM 1978 TO 1985

In 1978, American President **Jimmy Carter** hosted successful peace talks between Egypt and Israel at **Camp David**. The next year, however, a fundamentalist Islamist regime would take power in Iran, and many Americans would be taken hostage, only released upon the election of **Ronald Reagan**. Between 1980 and 1988, Iran and Iraq engaged in a bloody and brutal war, begun when the Iraqi leader **Saddam Hussein** seized territory in eastern Iran. Also, during this period, Afghan rebels were engaged in a prolonged, ultimately successful fight for independence from the Soviets. In 1982, Israel attacked Lebanon, which was harboring the Palestinian leader **Yasser Arafat**. Lebanon would be forced to oust Arafat the next year. Israel would continue attacking Arafat and the **Palestinian Liberation Organization**, and the PLO would continue to sponsor terrorist activities against Israel.

MIDDLE EAST FROM 1987 TO 2003

In 1987, Syrian troops entered Lebanon and stopped the civil war. Also, during this year, 402 pilgrims died during riots in the Saudi Arabian sacred city of Mecca. In 1988, the Palestinian resistance (known as the Intifada) began in earnest against Israel. Iraq invaded Kuwait in 1990, and after UN sanctions were levied, the US invaded in 1991. The Iraqi soldiers set fire to thousands of Kuwaiti oil wells while retreating. In 1992, Arafat and Israeli PM Yitzhak Rabin shook hands in Washington, and Arafat would soon return to Gaza after years of exile. In 1995, the Israelis and Palestinians signed an agreement giving the Palestinians autonomy in the West Bank and Gaza areas. Despite continuing violence, another agreement was reached in 1998, this one stating that the Palestinians would be granted land in exchange for keeping the peace. Violence continued, however, and in 2003, Israel began construction of a barrier between itself and the Palestinian territories.

NEW EUROPE AFTER 1991 THROUGH 1998

In 1991, **Gorbachev** resigned as the last president of the USSR, and a number of the Soviet provinces, including Lithuania and Latvia, declared independence. The **Maastricht Treaty**, formally announcing the creation of the European Union, was signed in 1992, and the next year a unified European stock market opened. In the **"Velvet" Revolution of 1993**, Slovakia separated from Czechoslovakia, which became the Czech Republic. Meanwhile, the former USSR was enduring civil strife until **Boris Yeltsin** seized power in 1993. In 1994, Russian troops attacked **Chechnya**, which was trying to achieve independence. In 1998, President Clinton helped broker a peace agreement between the **British** and **North Irish rebels**.

NEW EUROPE AFTER 1999

In 1999, the Czech Republic, Poland, and Hungary all joined **NATO**, further eliminating the old divides between western and eastern Europe. The conflict in Chechnya increased during this year, and Yeltsin was succeeded as Russian leader by the former KGB agent Vladimir Putin. An **International Criminal Court** was created in the Hague (Netherlands) in 2002, despite the vehement opposition of the United States. In the late '90s, many of the western European governments had become quasi-socialist, and they spent much of their time debating the immense increase in **immigration**. Meanwhile, the former Soviet states have had a rough transition from command to market economies, and are still somewhat economically depressed.

EMERGENCE OF THE PACIFIC RIM AFTER 1991

In the 1990s and early years of the 21st century, Japan and China emerged as two major economic powers. Despite suffering a prolonged recession, **Japan** continued to be one of the world's manufacturing leaders. However, several internal scandals have shaken Japanese confidence and have caused many to question the close relations between corporations and government. In **China**, the suffocating communist regime has relaxed its economic strictures somewhat, and the result has been an economic boom. China created several **special economic zones** along its eastern coast to lure foreign business. Now however, Chinese firms are control a sizable portion of the market in their own right.

FIRST WORLD, SECOND WORLD, AND THIRD WORLD

First-world nations are those that have advanced capitalist economies and are fully industrialized. The former Soviet states, which are slowly developing capitalist economies after having inefficient socialist economies for so long, are classified as **second-world nations**. This term has fallen out of general use, as these nations have slowly become more similar to first-world nations. The relatively poor and non-industrialized nations of Latin America, Africa, and Asia, most of which were colonized or involved in other exploitative trade arrangements with the Western empires at one time, are known as the **third-world nations**. Although these nations are far more numerous than those of the first or second world, they wield much less political power.Underdevelopment

Third-world countries that do not have the modern economic conditions possessed by the wealthier nations are said to suffer from **underdevelopment**. That is, they do not have the industrial, social, or political strength that is required to be a self-sustaining party in the global economy. In some countries, underdevelopment is clearly the result of **dysfunctional politics**; third-world nations are more likely to be ruled by a small group or by a dictator. Underdeveloped nations are typically those that were colonized at one time. Because their economy during the colonial period was so heavily based upon exporting raw materials, they never created a manufacturing base and found themselves unequipped for independence. Experts are at odds as to whether first-world nations should aid underdeveloped countries by funneling money to them or by helping them to develop modern economies.

SPECIFIC TECHNOLOGICAL ADVANCES SINCE 1991

In 1993, the first **web browser** was developed, beginning the era of internet communications that has revolutionized every area of human life. The internet did not become widely used, however, until 1997 and 1998. In 1997, a Scottish lab successfully **cloned** a lamb from adult sheep DNA, opening the door to the cloning of other animals, or human organs for medical purposes, and even for the cloning of entire human beings. This last possibility was strengthened in 2001, when the work of **sequencing the DNA** of the human genome was finally finished. Although **embryonic stem-cell research** has been limited in the US (other sources than embryos remain legal), other countries are using cells from human embryos to search for cures for disease. Another leap in genetic technology came in 2012 with the advent of CRISPR, a tool for directly editing the genes of any organism. In 2008, a new technology was used to implement Bitcoin called blockchain. This is a powerful method for sharing and storing information in an incredibly secure way, among many other uses. One of the most astonishing acheivements in science in recent history was in 2016 when the LIGO observatory used incredibly sensitive detectors to sense gravitational waves from distant colliding black holes.

MODERNIZATION

Modernization is the process by which societies develop sophisticated industrial technology, as well as the political, cultural, and social systems that are most effective in sustaining and advancing that technology. For a long time, sociologists noted that the most modernized countries, namely the Western empires, were the most successful, and that other societies should strive to emulate them. In recent decades, however, more sensitive sociologists have declared that **modernization** need not be equated with Westernization, and that the indigenous cultures of South America and Africa, for example, need not be cast off for these places to enjoy prosperity. One way sociologists can assess the relative modernization of a society is by comparing the **gross national product** (GNP), which is the total value of all economic activity within a society. Often, GNP is divided by total population to determine a society's **per capita gross national product**.

STATE THEORY OF MODERNIZATION AND WORLD SYSTEM THEORY OF MODERNIZATION

The state theory of modernization supports the ideals of **capitalism** by maintaining that whenever the government is restricted from seizing private property, capitalism will develop and free markets will arise as people modernize and strive to become more productive. The **world system theory of modernization**, also known as the **dependency theory**, states that some nations modernize at the expense of less-developed nations, and that so long as this exploitation continues, the less-developed nations will be unable to improve their lot. This theory essentially takes the **Marxist** view of the capitalist society, in which those who own the means of production are able to maintain dominance over the workers, and applies it to the interactions of nations.

GLOBALIZATION

Globalization is the process whereby all the social groups in the world are being brought into closer connection with one another. This has occurred mainly through the advances in transportation and communication technology, although the era of colonialism also had the effect of shrinking the world. This phenomenon has, in some cases, made it more difficult for repressive regimes to isolate themselves; during the Tiananmen Square uprising in China, for instance, Western media was able to communicate with the student rebels and present their story to the rest of the world. Many observers lament **globalization**, however, because they feel it will homogenize culture and crowd out fascinating, but not economically successful, societies.

> **Review Video: Globalization**
> Visit mometrix.com/academy and enter code: 551962

AUTOMATION

Automation is when machines are employed to do work formerly done by humans. This is typically done when an industry seeks to have greater worker productivity, but it may have some costly side effects. The work that remains for people after automation is frequently repetitive and mindless. Sociologists studying the phenomenon have observed increased alienation and lowered self-esteem among workers whose jobs have been automated. Also, automation reduces the need for specialization by driving employees out of their previously unique fields; this creates both unhealthy competition for menial jobs and confusion over social roles among the workers. Unfortunately, the pressures of the **capitalist market** make it impossible for most businesses to avoid automation.

Hyperurbanization

Hyperurbanization has occurred when the development of population growth in urban areas has moved too quickly and has outpaced the necessary accompanying growths in industry and business. The inevitable result of **hyperurbanization** is unemployment and inadequate public services. This has been a particular problem in **third-world countries**, which are experiencing mass internal migration from the countryside to the cities. In fact, the urbanization currently taking place in China may be the largest movement of people in the history of the world. It is impossible for any society, no matter how wealthy, to keep up with such a migration and provide adequate roads, health care, education, water, food, and electricity.

Chapter Quiz

Ready to see how well you retained what you just read? Scan the QR code to go directly to the chapter quiz interface for this study guide. If you're using a computer, simply visit the online resources page at **mometrix.com/resources719/apworldhistory-27797** and click the Chapter Quizzes link.

World History: Historiography

Transform passive reading into active learning! After immersing yourself in this chapter, put your comprehension to the test by taking a quiz. The insights you gained will stay with you longer this way. Scan the QR code to go directly to the chapter quiz interface for this study guide. If you're using a computer, simply visit the online resources page at **mometrix.com/resources719/apworldhistory-27797** and click the Chapter Quizzes link.

INTRODUCTION TO HISTORIOGRAPHY

Historiography is the study of the methods and approaches that historians use to create histories. It involves examining how historical evidence is chosen, interpreted, evaluated, analyzed, and used in the writing of history. Historiography is not concerned with the events that make up history but rather the manner in which that history was recorded. The sources, techniques, and theoretical frameworks used to record the history of a certain subject constitute that subject's historiography.

COMMON TERMINOLOGY USED WHEN STUDYING HISTORY

When studying history, it is important to have a clear understanding of various terms that can be used interchangeably. The term **time** refers to the continuous passing of events in the past, present, and future. Time is a scientific measure that conventionally uses minutes, hours, days, and years as its **standard measures**. Time passes with or without significant events taking place. **History** is distinct from time as it is the record of **significant events** throughout the past. The term **chronology** refers to the arrangement of events in their correct order. As history contains uncertainty, the chronology of particular events is up for debate. Terms used to describe the ebb and flow of history are change and continuity. **Continuity** refers to periods of time that are relatively stable in history with no major changes, whereas times of **change** refer to rich periods in history with significant events that alter the common practices of that time, often leading into a new era. When describing what has changed for a civilization over time, it is common to focus on political, economic, social, and technological aspects. For instance, the United States government was established in 1776 and continues today. This demonstrates a change at the beginning of the timeline related the United States, but since then, there has been political continuity as it has existed for roughly 250 years. Other aspects of life in this period may have experienced other changes, such as the innovation of electricity, steam engines, and automobiles. When a portion of time has relatively stable conditions such that it can be summed up by a common characterization, it is called a **period of time**; this process of summing up time into periods is called **periodization**.

CIVILIZATION, CITY-STATES, AND EMPIRES

Since history is the study of recorded events throughout time, it is naturally tied to organized society with a developed language to record the events. The development necessary to record history generally coincides with early civilization. A **civilization** is a human society that has established complex means of surviving as a group. These **functions** are developing a food supply, a social structure, a shared language, a culture, and technology. The first known complex civilization is Mesopotamia, which was more easily developed due to its fertile farmlands, access to water through an available river. Mesopotamia is a good example of a **city-state**, which is essentially an independently sovereign city that does not depend on another government. Mesopotamia, as an early civilization, was the central hub and government in its region. The model of city-states still exists today, though they are often comparatively less significant in size and economy compared to other nation-states. Examples of modern city-states include Monaco, Vatican City, and Singapore. As the early civilizations continued to develop, they would eventually grow into **empires**, which are larger sovereign states with multiple territories, though they are usually governed centrally by a monarch or emperor.

INTERPRETING TIMELINES

Timelines are a useful tool for visualizing the chronology of events as well as a great method to map out periods and view changes or continuity throughout history. Timelines can focus on either small or large ranges and can be multifaceted so that one period or type of event can be compared with another. A key element of a timeline is having a consistent interval mapped out. For instance, if we wanted to construct a timeline to map the events that happened for a single day, we would likely use hours to plot out the continuum. One might start the timeline at 12am and end the timeline at 12am the next night to show the picture of the entire day. Each event or period, such as sleeping, waking up, eating, going to work, and special occurrences can be marked on the timeline to plot out the day. If someone wanted to compare multiple days, these timelines could be lined up and compared and contrasted to find what is common to all days and what is unique. These same concepts can be applied to historical timelines as well. Instead of mapping just one day, one might consider mapping the events leading up to and throughout a particular war. The significance of events should change with the focus of the timeline. Seeing events plotted on a steady continuum of time can be very helpful in understanding the pacing of events throughout history.

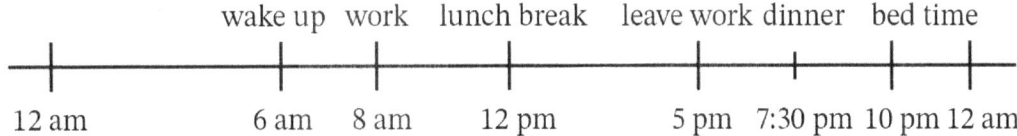

RELATIONSHIPS BETWEEN HISTORICAL EVENTS AND THEIR IMPLICATIONS

As one aspect of society changes, it frequently proves to have significant effects on other parts of society. One of the easiest ways to see this effect is the innovation of new technologies. An example of a highly impactful technology is the printing press. Prior to this invention, all written documents had to be written by hand, which was time-consuming and costly. Books were very expensive and rare, which put the burden of education on mainly religious authorities and very wealthy classes of people. This new innovation allowed for more written works to be spread, which caused a need for literacy and education, ultimately evoking huge cultural and political changes. Technology tends to be a much quicker influencer of change in civilization, as it is sudden and can have dramatic impacts on how things are done. Cultural, political, and economic effects tend to move more gradually but likewise have strong effects that can change civilization forever.

PRIMARY AND SECONDARY SOURCES OF HISTORICAL INFORMATION

When studying history, it is important to consider the reliability, validity, and availability of sources of information. **Primary sources** are first-hand accounts of an event, such as a transcript of a speech, a recording, statistics, or a work of art. **Secondary sources** are indirect records, such as text books, newspapers, and other forms of reviews of the primary sources. Secondary sources of information can still be valid and useful, but are more open to **interpretation** and **bias**. Information from recent history, such as the election of a president in the 2010s is very reliable, as there are many sources of information that are in consensus about the objective event. Furthermore, many people still alive are primary sources since they were alive and witnessed the election. This is not true of less modern history, such as the election of Abraham Lincoln in 1860. There are still plentiful records of the information, but all witnesses to the election have passed away at this point. This event took place in an era where newspapers and legitimate documentation was widespread and available. The clarity and objectivity of sources are indisputable because they are so abundant. If, however, we only had political cartoons and election campaign brochures to go by, the reliability and accuracy of the information may be up for debate because the source materials are only secondary sources of information and are likely to contain biases. Generally, the further back in history one researches, the fewer sources are available due to lack of documentation, technological limitations, and language barriers. With fewer sources, and possibly conflicting information, historians must put together the most reasonable explanation of what took place during the period in question, given the amount of information available to them.

Types of Sources of Information Used in Historical Research

- **Almanacs**—books that are published each year to express current information for consideration in the coming year. These often act as time capsules for that particular year and can give historians insight into economic and technological details of the time.
- **Encyclopedias**—resources that cover a variety of topics broadly for the purpose of giving the reader an overview. Wikipedia is an internet-based version of an encyclopedia that is useful for finding leads or obtaining general information about a topic.
- **Bibliographies**—a list of resources used in composing a scholarly work. These are usually primary and secondary sources that can be used to check an author's sources or to give leads on similar research. Similar concepts include works-cited pages and literature reviews.
- **Periodical Guides**—a series of publications over time, usually in the form of magazines or journals. These usually broach a more specific category of information, such as on research methods, psychology, or medical procedures, and are intended to help members of a particular field stay up-to-date with current research in their field.
- **Biographical Dictionaries**—a resource that contains a list of important names to know about the given subject and a description of how they contributed to the field. For instance, if one were interested in the Revolutionary War, a biographical dictionary would include information on each of the founding fathers and other significant individuals of the time.
- **Maps**—representations of land and territories that can display a variety of factors, including geographical features, political features, economics, demographics, and many more aspects. Digital maps can generally be manipulated to show multiple features at once.

Uses and Limitations of Various Historical Source Materials

Historical source materials are a type of primary source material that offer historians the opportunity to study people, places, and events that occurred in the past. Unfortunately, there are limitations to what these materials can tell us. A limitation of **historical source materials** is that they may be biased by those who created them. For example, those who create historical documents such as letters may leave out details or exaggerate parts in order to make their points more convincing. Another limitation might be that some historical sources only provide evidence for certain points of view, as they were recorded by those with specific interests and perspectives.

- An **oral history** provides an account of an event that happened in the past, which is told by the person who was there when it happened. Oral histories are important because they allow us to learn about things that may not be written in books or recorded in documents.
- **Newspapers** are important source materials for scholars because they provide a detailed account of the past, which cannot be found in books or other sources. Newspapers are not always reliable as they may not be based on fact, while others might omit certain information or give undue weight towards one side of an issue at the expense of another.

- **Diaries** and personal **journals** can provide valuable information for historians because they are detailed histories of people's lives. However, the reliability of these accounts is always in question because they were created by just one person and aren't always written with the intention of sharing.
- **Artifacts** can be defined as objects created by humans, which can give hints at the peoples' material culture and intangible culture. Material culture includes things like buildings or furniture while intangible culture includes things like music or dance. The benefits of artifacts are that they can offer insights into how people lived in the past. They can also be used to shed light on the thoughts, feelings, fears, tensions, customs, rituals, and other social practices at that time.
- **Tax lists** and **census data** are useful sources of insight into how people lived during a certain time. They provide us with reliable information about the income, demographics, and beliefs of the people living in a particular time.
- **Personal correspondence** has been an important form of historical information for historians. It gives an insight into the lives and interactions of ordinary people. The main benefits of using personal correspondence as a source for history is that it provides an authentic portrayal of the author's thoughts and feelings during a time period or in response to significant events.

HISTORICAL INTERPRETATION AND BIASES

History is a discipline that relies on the interpretation of **facts** to create **narratives**. Due to the types and availability of sources, history tends to leave itself open to **subjectivity**. Often, this means that **biases** are introduced at either the source of information, the interpretation of the information, or at the explanation of the information. For instance, if the only **sources of information** about an event are newspapers, the author of these historical sources may have been biased, causing the **interpretation** of the actual events to be skewed from the start. Similarly, the person interpreting the source may have their own biases that they introduce or even **teach** to others in the process of communicating the historical narrative. Commonly described biases in modern interpretation of history generally revolve around sociopolitical issues such as Eurocentrism, popular political parties, economic biases, and cultural favoritism.

HISTORICAL REVISIONISM

Historical revisionism is the act of reinterpreting a historical account through established historical methodologies. This is often done when new information is discovered or old information is reinterpreted in such a way that it warrants reconsidering the previously accepted history of an event or period. Historical revisionism is an essential and necessary process in creating accurate histories. Revisionism can, sometimes, be used incorrectly and in a way that leads to a less accurate interpretation of historical events. An example of this would be when the historical record is denied or deliberately distorted. This can involve using falsified records, purposefully misrepresenting the meaning of a piece of historical evidence, manipulating statistics, or unjustly denying the validity of historical evidence. A common example of this is Holocaust denial, which is an antisemitic theory that the Holocaust was either fabricated or greatly exaggerated.

Chapter Quiz

Ready to see how well you retained what you just read? Scan the QR code to go directly to the chapter quiz interface for this study guide. If you're using a computer, simply visit the online resources page at **mometrix.com/resources719/apworldhistory-27797** and click the Chapter Quizzes link.

AP Practice Test #1

Want to take this practice test in an online interactive format? Check out the online resources page, which includes interactive practice questions and much more: **mometrix.com/resources719/apworldhistory-27797**

1. In the American Progressive movement, which of these professions stimulated reform?
   a. Pragmatist educators
   b. Muckraking journalists
   c. Psychologists and sociologists
   d. Novelists writing fictional works
   e. All of these professions caused reform

Refer to the following for question 2:

> My name is Amorosa. I am fourteen years old and I live near the Gulf Coast in South Texas. My father runs an oil refinery and my mother is a schoolteacher. I have two brothers, named Jorge and Emil—they are sixteen-year-old twins! After school, when there is no soccer practice, I love to spend time in the Art classroom. I love the paints, clays, fabrics, and other materials used to create beautiful things. Next year, my family and friends will celebrate my Quinceañera, a large party in honor of my 15th birthday. There will be music, food, a Court of Honor made up of my friends, and most importantly, a beautiful dress. In my city, there are talented women who design and make ball gowns that we will wear. When I celebrate my Quinceañera, I will help the dress designer create my dress.

2. How could Amorosa's teacher encourage her to use her interests to build her understanding of various cultural influences and diversity?
   a. Ask Amorosa to bring in pictures of all of the events surrounding the celebration to show her classmates.
   b. Encourage Amorosa to research similar customs in other cultures present in Texas (e.g., Swiss, French, Native American) and compare and contrast them.
   c. Require Amorosa to speak to her class about what her family's heritage means to her and how her culture has influenced the person she has become.
   d. Allow Amorosa to use her artistic skills to teach so that she can work with children of all ages and backgrounds.

3. What did the Iconoclasts oppose?
   a. The elevation of religious leaders to powerful positions.
   b. The use of religious images in worship.
   c. The worship of saints.
   d. The worship of the Mother Mary.
   e. The watering-down of Christianity for the illiterate.

4. Which American city did the Dutch East India Company purchase in 1626 and name New Amsterdam?
    a. Charleston.
    b. New York City.
    c. New Orleans.
    d. Boston.
    e. Philadelphia.

5. Which of the following is NOT a way that the Internet has affected worldwide economies?
    a. It made near instantaneous communication possible.
    b. It caused an overall increase in the cost of transactions.
    c. It increased consumer access to goods.
    d. It increased the barriers to entry in retail situations.

6. Which of the following is a correct statement concerning the French and Indian War?
    a. Then-Major George Washington, dispatched to Pennsylvania to oust the French, succeeded.
    b. In 1756, this war extended over to Europe, where it became known as the Seven Years' War.
    c. Colonial delegates included Thomas Jefferson, who proposed an intercolonial government.
    d. English Major General Edward Braddock defeated an ambush on the way to Fort Duquesne.
    e. The Treaty of Paris gave Britain all France's territories in Canada, but not in all of North America.

7. How does the prevalence of ziggurats in ancient Mesopotamia illustrate a central factor of Mesopotamian culture?
    a. Intended as lookouts, the number of ziggurats illustrates a Mesopotamian concern for security from invaders.
    b. Used for stargazing, the number of ziggurats shows how Mesopotamian culture depended on astrology.
    c. Dedicated to Mesopotamian rulers, the ziggurats illustrate the complete control Mesopotamian kings held over their subjects.
    d. Structures dedicated to gods, the ziggurats illustrate the importance of religion in Mesopotamian culture.

8. Which of the following statements is *incorrect* regarding England's Glorious Revolution?
    a. One outcome of this revolution was the crowning of William and Mary as leaders.
    b. One outcome of the revolution was Parliament's writing an English Bill of Rights.
    c. One reason that this revolution occurred was fighting between Whigs and Tories.
    d. One reason that this revolution was called "glorious" was its minimal casualties.
    e. The English Bill of Rights influenced America's Constitution and Bill of Rights.

Refer to the following for question 9:

Between May 15 and June 25 of 1919, more than 30,000 Canadian workers walked off the job in what became known as the Winnipeg General Strike of 1919. This labour action was fueled by high rates of unemployment caused by soldiers returning from military service after the end of the First World War (also known as the Great War) in 1918, as well as high inflation. For many workers, benefits were few, hours were long, and dangerous working conditions were common. The business community remained strongly opposed to unionization or collective bargaining, which further increased the growing frustration among many workers and the unemployed.

Prior to the general strike, workers in several unions in the city of Winnipeg had been negotiating for improvements in their working conditions, the right to collective bargaining, and better pay. On May 1, 1919, the Winnipeg builders' and metal workers' unions went on strike. Two weeks later, on May 15, the Winnipeg Trades and Labour Council (WTLC) called for a general strike of all workers across the city. The first solidarity strike was from the Winnipeg telephone operators, or as they were often called, the "Hello Girls." Within hours, nearly 30,000 people had walked off the job in a strike action, resulting in factories, businesses and public services being forced to close. Public sector workers, including police officers, firefighters, and telephone and utilities operators, also participated in the general strike.

Fearing that the movement could spread to other cities, the federal government intervened to end the strike. Parliament amended the Immigration Act so that British-born strike leaders could be deported, and the Criminal Code was modified to broaden the definition of sedition. The federal government threatened to fire all federal public servants who refused to return to work immediately. Meanwhile, the city of Winnipeg fired much of the police force and hired 1,800 special constables. The "specials" were each provided with a horse and a baseball bat and given instructions to end the strike. In response, a riot broke out on June 10. A few days later, 12 union leaders were arrested, and the publication of a pro-strike newspaper was prohibited. A large protest was organized in support of the arrested leaders, which led to acts of vandalism. RCMP and military forces arrested many protesters, leading to the deaths of two individuals and at least 30 injuries. This day came to be known as "Bloody Saturday." The strike ended with soldiers occupying the streets of Winnipeg.

While the strike did not immediately result in gains for the workers, it did, over time, result in lasting changes as workers in cities across Canada demanded action. The Co-operative Commonwealth Federation (CCF) was founded by former strikers, many of whom were elected at the municipal, provincial and federal levels. The CCF later formed government in the province of Saskatchewan, and its successor party, the New Democratic Party (NDP), continues to routinely hold government in several Canadian provinces.

9. Which of the following were lasting consequences of the ending of the General Strike?
a. The city of Winnipeg no longer has a regular police force.
b. A new political party and movement achieved greater success in several provinces.
c. Canada is able to deport unwanted British labour activists.
d. Inflation and high prices for consumer goods continue to be a problem in Winnipeg.
e. Strikes would become much less common in Canada over the long term.

10. Which of the following is a long-term consequence of the development of trade along the Silk Road which still impacts the world to this day?
a. The Silk Road came to an end in the 1450s as a result of the Ottoman Empire intentionally forcing trade routes with the East to be closed.
b. The Mongol Expansion permanently established Mongolia as a key international power until the 20th century.
c. Religions spread from East to West, and West to East.
d. The Chinese Han dynasty achieved victory in the War of the Heavenly Horses.
e. Trade increased between the Chinese Empire and the Parthian Empire.

11. **Which of the following statements does NOT describe the average European diet before the expansion of trade routes?**
    a. Europeans ate for survival, not enjoyment.
    b. They had an abundance of preservatives such as salt that could make food last longer.
    c. Grain-based foods such as porridge and bread were staple meals.
    d. Spices were unavailable.

12. **Which of the following choices most recently controlled a majority of India?**
    a. The Gupta Dynasty
    b. The Maurya Empire
    c. The Mughal Empire
    d. The Maratha Empire

13. **Which of the following does NOT represent a major threat to the Amazon rainforest?**
    a. Industrial development
    b. Highway construction
    c. Scientific research
    d. Logging interests

14. **Carrie Chapman Catt founded the League of Women Voters in 1920 in response to which of the following historical events?**
    a. The election of President Woodrow Wilson.
    b. The passage of the Nineteenth Amendment to the Constitution.
    c. The breakup of the National Women's Party.
    d. The end of World War I.

15. **The Dred Scott case involved the Supreme Court ruling on**
    a. Women's voting rights
    b. Civil rights
    c. Miranda Rights
    d. Right to an attorney

16. **What were Martin Luther's 95 theses?**
    a. His charter for the Lutheran Church
    b. Criticisms of practices in the Catholic Church
    c. A document explaining his differences with other Protestant churches
    d. Reasons why the Bible should be translated into popular languages.

17. **Who were the Shoguns?**
    a. Chinese military leaders
    b. Japanese military leaders
    c. Chinese religious leaders
    d. Japanese religious leaders

18. Which of the following is not true about affirmative action?
    a. In the case of *Bakke v. University of California*, the Supreme Court upheld affirmative action.
    b. Affirmative action in the 1960s tried to raise black representation to approximate racial balance.
    c. White critics contended that affirmative action backfired by engendering reverse discrimination.
    d. Following *Bakke v. University of California*, Supreme Court rulings mitigated affirmative action.
    e. All of these statements are true with respect to events associated with affirmative action programs.

19. Which of the following is not true regarding the Korean War?
    a. Fighting between Chinese Nationalists and Communists existed before World War II.
    b. Truman's administration would not recognize Mao's new People's Republic of China.
    c. The United Nations Security Council approved the US bid for military intervention.
    d. General MacArthur's invasion of Inchon on September 15, 1950, was not successful.
    e. Armistice discussions began in July, 1951, but the war did not end until July, 1953.

20. Which of the following is NOT true regarding the early colonization of New York?
    a. Dutch fur traders first created the New Amsterdam settlement on Manhattan Island in 1624.
    b. King Charles II of England entitled his brother James to conquer New Amsterdam in 1664.
    c. James, Duke of York, prohibited assemblies in New York as he was against representation.
    d. Colonel Richard Nicols granted very few civil or political rights to the New York colonials.
    e. New York colonial citizens, especially Puritans on Long Island, demanded self-government.

21. What did the Scientific Revolution emphasize?
    a. Tradition and authority
    b. Observation and reason
    c. Superstition
    d. Theology

22. Which of the following written works did Thomas Paine publish *after* the American Revolution?
    a. Common Sense
    b. Rights of Man
    c. The Age of Reason
    d. Rights of Man and The Age of Reason
    e. None of the above

23. The Maastricht Treaty of 1992 removed many of the economic and political barriers that existed among members of which of the following groups?
    a. United Nations
    b. North Atlantic Treaty Organization
    c. European Union
    d. Organization of Petroleum Exporting Countries

24. In 1955 the Soviet Union formed the Warsaw Treaty Organization to counterbalance which of the following?
   a. NAFTA
   b. NATO
   c. The U.N. Security Counsel
   d. The Four Power Pact

25. Of the following, which statement about the US economy in the 1990s is correct?
   a. By the year 2000, the US economy was increasing at a rate of 5% a year.
   b. The rate of unemployment in America at this time dropped to 6%.
   c. The rates of productivity and of inflation in the US were about the same.
   d. The US stock market's total value had doubled in only six years.

26. Of the following countries, which did NOT experience more war soon after World War II?
   a. Greece
   b. China
   c. Korea
   d. Japan

27. Which of the following is true about the Eightieth Congress during the Truman administration?
   a. Congress approved the Taft-Hartley Act in 1947 after President Truman agreed to it.
   b. The Taft-Hartley Act allowed workplaces to restrict employees to union members.
   c. Congress raised farm aid and passed bills for health insurance and minimum wages.
   d. Truman promoted his "Fair Deal," but bipartisan Southern congressmen foiled it.
   e. American voters' approval of Congressional acts ensured the reelection of Truman.

28. How did the Crusader army that went on the First Crusade differ from the Crusader armies that Pope Urban II envisioned?
   a. There was no difference. The people of Europe were accustomed to obeying clerical direction and eagerly joined the cause. They created an army that was primarily made up of faithful Christians from all social classes led by a select group of knights who were responsible for leading and training their armies.
   b. There was no difference. The people of Europe obeyed clerical direction and stayed home to pray for the success of an army composed entirely of knights and other professional military personnel.
   c. Pope Urban II had envisioned an army of skilled knights and professional soldiers; instead, men and women from all classes joined together to retake the Holy Land.
   d. Pope Urban II had envisioned an army composed of faithful Christians from all social classes led by a group of select knights; instead, the army was primarily made up of knights and other professional military personnel.

29. The first coin-based economy was established by which of the following people?
   a. Phoenicians.
   b. Egyptians.
   c. Hebrews.
   d. Lydians.
   e. Babylonians.

30. On July 1, 1867, three British colonies united to form the Dominion of Canada. These three colonies were the Province of Canada (consisting of Ontario and Quebec), New Brunswick, and Nova Scotia. Since then, six more provinces and three territories have joined Canada. What was the process and product of this union called?
    a. Confederation
    b. Unification
    c. Federalization
    d. Ratification
    e. Decentralization

31. Which of these statements is inaccurate regarding the Dutch Republic in the 17th century?
    a. The Dutch Republic was centrally governed by its strongest province, Holland.
    b. During the 17th century, the Dutch had great naval and economic world powers.
    c. At that time, the Dutch were trading in Asia, Africa, North America and the Caribbean.
    d. Religious tolerance and the Dutch Golden Age in artwork were hallmarks of the time.
    e. Amsterdam was a world banking center; Grotius and others formed the center of international free trade.

32. Which of the following statements about immigration to the United States from 2000-2005 is incorrect?
    a. Less immigration to the United States occurred in these years than in other years.
    b. More immigration to the United States occurred in these years than in other years.
    c. There was greater border security in the United States after the 9/11 attacks.
    d. Almost eight million persons immigrated to the US at this time.

33. Which of the following statements correctly identifies the source of the term "Indians" for Native American peoples?
    a. It is a translation of a tribal word meaning "people of the land"
    b. It is a variation of the term "aborigine" that changed over time
    c. It refers to the fact that these people first migrated from India
    d. It is a synonym for the word "indigenous" that means "native"
    e. It refers to Columbus' erroneous thinking that he found the West Indies

34. What does the Communist Manifesto claim makes up all of history?
    a. Battles between political ideas
    b. Class struggles
    c. Battles to control the means of production
    d. None of the above

Refer to the following for question 35:

35. What viewpoint is the creator of this cartoon most likely expressing regarding Sir John A. MacDonald's National Policy?

   a. The National Policy would likely fail, as Canadian farmers and Canadian mechanics would consume all the profits, thereby causing American manufacturers to be shut out of the market.
   b. The National Policy would likely succeed, as Canadian workers and American manufacturers would each benefit.
   c. Sir John A. MacDonald would benefit more from the success of the National Policy than would Canadian or American manufacturing.
   d. The National Policy would result in higher profits for Canadian farmers and mechanics, and the only group to lose would be American manufacturers.
   e. The National Policy would likely contribute to the growing trade deficit between Canada and the United States.

36. Which of the following statements is NOT true about slavery in America?

   a. The Spanish brought African slaves to Florida by the 1560s.
   b. Chattel (ownership) slavery was legal in America from 1654 to 1865.
   c. Indentured servants preceded slavery in America as sources of labor.
   d. Southern colonies imported more slaves in the 1600s to farm cotton.

37. Regarding the Treaty of Westphalia, all but which of these is factual?
    a. It politically recognized the Swiss Confederacy (Switzerland) as independent.
    b. It politically recognized the United Provinces of Holland as independent.
    c. It accomplished the preparation for the politics in Europe to become secularized.
    d. It provided for reparations to France, which had undergone severe war damages.
    e. It was met with opposition by the Pope, but it was nonetheless signed.

38. Which of these is *not* a consequence of the British Empire?
    a. The freedom that is currently found in America
    b. The freedom that is currently found in Jamaica
    c. Problems of hostile groups that coexist in India
    d. Problems of hostile groups in African countries
    e. The freedom that currently exists in Hong Kong

39. Which of the following statements is not true of daily life for the average European in the 1500s?
    a. Life was not significantly different from the medieval era.
    b. The majority of people worked in agriculture.
    c. Life expectancy was short.
    d. Most people were literate, due to well-financed public education programs.
    e. The Commercial Revolution and the colonization of new lands made new opportunities possible for the first time.

40. During the decolonization of the Cold War years, which of the following events occurred chronologically latest?
    a. The Eastern Bloc and Satellite states became independent from the Soviet Union.
    b. Canada became totally independent from British Parliament via the Canada Act.
    c. The Bahamas, in the Caribbean, became independent from the United Kingdom.
    d. The Algerian War ended, and Algeria became independent from France.

41. Which of the following battles persuaded France to enter America's war against Britain?
    a. The Battle of Saratoga
    b. The Battle of Brandywine Creek
    c. The Battle of Oriskany
    d. The Battle of Bennington
    e. None of the above

Refer to the following for question 42:

Women in the Labor Force, Selected Years

Year	Women in Labor Force (thousands)	Percentage of Total Labor Force
1900	5,114	18.1
1920	8,430	20.4
1940	12,845	24.3
1950	18,412	28.8
1970	31,560	36.7

42. In what year did women first make up more than 25% of the total labor force?
    a. 1900
    b. 1920
    c. 1940
    d. 1950

43. In which country does a large part of the native, traditionally nomadic people currently live in large tents known as yurts or gers?
    a. Indonesia
    b. Mongolia
    c. Thailand
    d. India

44. Which of the following statements is *not* true regarding English expansionism in the 16th century?
    a. England's defeat of the Spanish Armada in 1588 brought a decisive end to their war with Spain.
    b. King Henry VIII's desire to divorce Catherine of Aragon strengthened English expansionism.
    c. Queen Elizabeth's support for the Protestant Reformation strengthened English expansionism.
    d. Sir Francis Drake and other English sea captains plundered the goods that the Spaniards took from indigenous peoples.
    e. Sir Francis Drake's voyages to and conquests of new territories were supported by Elizabeth.

45. Which of the following kingdoms was not part of the unification of the Iberian Peninsula now known as Spain?
    a. Aragon.
    b. Castile.
    c. Granada.
    d. Kiev.
    e. Navarre.

46. A monotheistic religious practice was central to which of the following cultures?
    a. Egyptians.
    b. Hebrews.
    c. Sumerians.
    d. Babylonians.
    e. Hittites.

47. How did Russia's participation in World War I influence the Russian Revolution?
a. Civilian suffering and military setbacks served as a catalyst for revolutionary forces.
b. Nicholas III capitalized on battlefield successes to temporarily silence critics.
c. The government eased laws banning collective action by factory workers to appease social discontent about the war.
d. Anti-government protesters temporarily ceased protesting to show patriotism in a difficult war.

48. Of the following men who contributed to the automotive industry in the 19th and 20th centuries, which one was *not* specifically an inventor, developer, or manufacturer of engines and/or cars?
a. Karl Benz
b. Henry Ford
c. Rudolf Diesel
d. Gottlieb Daimler
e. John

49. To whom was the Declaration of Independence addressed and why?
a. To the British Parliament because the colonists were opposed to being ruled by a king who had only inherited his throne and only considered the popularly elected Parliament to hold any authority over them
b. To the King of England because the colonists were upset that Parliament was passing laws for them even though they did not have the right to elect members of Parliament to represent their interests
c. To the governors of the rebelling colonies so that they would know that they had 30 days to either announce their support of the Revolution or to return to England
d. To the colonial people as a whole because the Declaration of Independence was intended to outline the wrongs that had been inflicted on them by the British military and inspire them to rise up in protest

50. Which of the following was *not* one of the scandals associated with corruption that existed during Grant's presidency?
a. The Black Friday Scandal
b. The Salary Grab
c. The Whiskey Ring Fraud
d. The bribing of Belknap
e. All of the above scandals occurred during Grant's presidency.

51. Which of the following is NOT true about the English Civil Wars between 1641 and 1651?
a. These wars all were waged between Royalists and Parliamentarians
b. The outcome of this series of civil wars was victory for Parliament
c. These wars legalized Parliament's consent as requisite to monarchy
d. Two of the wars in this time involved supporters of King Charles I
e. One of the wars in this time involved supporters of King Charles II

52. The Renaissance which began in Italy subsequently spread to which of the following other countries in Europe?
   a. All of these
   b. France
   c. Germany
   d. England
   e. Poland

53. In England, the population of the city of London alone increased by ___ times from 1800 to 1900.
   a. two and a half
   b. three and a half
   c. four and a half
   d. five and a half
   e. six and a half

54. Which of the following was NOT an immediate effect of rapid urban growth in the 1800s?
   a. Poor sanitation conditions in the cities
   b. Epidemics of diseases in the cities
   c. Inadequate police and fire protection
   d. Widespread urban political corruption

55. Which of the following is not a true statement concerning the beginnings of slavery in the Virginia colony?
   a. Slavery was established quickly as a means of securing a cheap source of labor.
   b. Initially slaves could become free through converting to Christianity.
   c. The number of slaves in Virginia increased as tobacco planters required a steady supply of labor.
   d. Early Virginian slaves included both Africans and Native Americans.

Answer Key and Explanations for Test #1

1. E: All of these professions caused reform in the American Progressive movement. Progressivism had its foundations in Pragmatist philosophy. Famous educator (a) John Dewey was one of the people who developed this philosophy, as was William James, the philosopher and great pioneer of psychology (c). They both largely influenced Progressive thought. Journalists known as muckrakers (b) exposed corruption and other social ills. For example, Ida Tarbell exposed the practices of the Standard Oil Company; Lincoln Steffens exposed local government corruption in his 1904 book, The Shame of the Cities; and in 1908, Ray Stannard Baker exposed negative race relations in Following the Color Line. Nonfiction journalists were not the only writers to inspire reform. Novelists also exposed cultural problems in need of reform by placing such cultural problems in fictionalized contexts (d). Theodore Dreiser (perhaps most famous for his 1900 novel Sister Carrie) penned two novels, The Financier in 1912 and The Titan in 1914, portraying characters who were ruthless businessmen. Upton Sinclair published his novel, The Jungle, in 1906, painting a realistic picture of meatpacking plants so effective that landmark laws were passed to improve conditions (i.e. the Meat Inspection Act and the Pure Food and Drug Act). In addition to early psychologists such as William James, sociologists (c) also contributed to Progressive reforms. Lester Frank Ward published Dynamic Sociology in 1883, defining the Progressive movement's philosophical bases and criticizing contrasting laissez-faire policies. In 1899, Thorstein Veblen published The Theory of the Leisure Class, in which he denigrated the "conspicuous consumption" of the most affluent members of society.

2. B: Students are more motivated to inquire and learn new things when the topic at hand is relevant to their real lives. Since Amorosa is obviously looking forward to her *Quinceañera,* she may enjoy researching similar celebrations and customs inherent in other cultures. By relating this cultural research to an event, she is anticipating, her teacher will help her identify relevant similarities across many cultures. Amorosa will also have an opportunity to practice understanding contrasts between various events as well as cultures throughout the project that will aid her in deepening cultural awareness in the future.

3. B: The iconoclasts opposed the use of religious images, or icons, in worship. Choice E does reflect part of the argument made by proponents of icons, namely that it helped to spread Christianity to the illiterate masses. By the 7th Century A.D., images of Jesus and the saints gained popularity for use in worship. Many Christians believed that the worship of images was a false form of religion. In the 8th Century, Emperor Leo III of Byzantium and Pope Adrian I outlawed the worship of icons. This decision eventually led to the split between the Roman Catholic and Eastern Orthodox Churches.

4. B: The Dutch East India Company named the region after the city of Amsterdam. The city was renamed after the British took control of the region in 1664.

5. B: The Internet has increased the number of methods in which near-instantaneous communication is possible, indirectly improving the economy by opening new channels for communication at great distances. The internet has also generally caused a decrease in transaction costs and barriers to entry in retail situations (e.g., it is much less expensive to start a website to sell your goods than it is to open a physical store). The Internet has also increased consumer access to goods by making it easier for consumers to locate what they want.

6. B: After fighting began in American in 1754, the war spread to Europe in 1756, where it was called the Seven Years' War. In America, it was called the French and Indian War. George Washington, who was then a major in the Virginia militia, was sent to Pennsylvania to expunge the French, but he was not successful (A). He initially won a skirmish, but his troops were outnumbered, so they retreated and then surrendered. Meanwhile, delegates came from seven of the colonies to meet in Albany, N.Y. to confer on defense plans. The delegate who proposed the idea of an intercolonial government (C) was Benjamin Franklin, not Thomas Jefferson. Though other colonial delegates did not agree, Franklin's idea is considered significant because it set a precedent for presenting a united front against a common enemy, something America did in later wars such as World Wars I and II. Major General Braddock of England was ambushed en route to Fort Duquesne (D), but he did not defeat the French and Indian fighters who ambushed his troops. Instead, Braddock and two thirds of the British troops were killed in this battle. In 1763, the Treaty of Paris ended the French and Indian War. As a result of this treaty, all of France's territories in Canada and the rest of North America were ceded to England (E).

7. D: Ziggurats were towers dedicated to gods; their prevalence indicates the importance of religion in Mesopotamian culture. The other options can be rejected because they pair accurate facts about Mesopotamia with inaccurate summaries of the purposes of the ziggurats. For example, while rulers of Mesopotamian cities fought among themselves, ziggurats were not used as lookouts. This eliminates option A. Although astrology was practiced in Mesopotamia, ziggurats did not function as places for stargazing or observing the sky. Finally, Mesopotamian cities were ruled by kings, but the ziggurats were not dedicated to them. This eliminates options B and C.

8. C: The Whigs and the Tories in England did disagree at one point, but by the advent of the Glorious Revolution, Whigs and Tories in Parliament agreed about the revolution. The Whigs had wanted to stop King Charles II's brother James II from succeeding to the throne because James was Catholic while the Tories supported Charles II. Once James II did succeed to the throne, he exempted Catholics from laws that had prevented them from serving in the armed forces, the court system, and local government. This led both Whigs and Tories in Parliament to reunite against what they saw as a common enemy: the reversion of England from Protestantism to Catholicism. Thus the Glorious Revolution was neither a conflict between Whigs and Tories nor a result of any such conflict. Parliament invited the Dutch Republic's William III of Orange, James II's nephew, and William's wife Mary, James' oldest daughter, to overtake the English throne. William accepted the offer and invaded England. This did lead to the crowning of William and Mary (A). Another result was the drafting by Parliament of the English Bill of Rights (B). One reason this revolution was called "glorious" was its minimal casualties (D). [Note: This revolution is often called "bloodless" which is not entirely accurate. However, compared to other revolutions, there were few battles, relatively little blood was shed, and few people died.] Since James ultimately fled the country, William's invasion met with little resistance. This revolution was also called "glorious" because it ended absolute rule in England and can be said to be the start of modern Parliamentary democracy in England. It is true that the English Bill of Rights influenced America's Constitution and Bill of Rights (E); in fact, it had a major influence on these documents: The English Bill of Rights prevented rulers from making laws without the approval of Parliament; the American counterpart to this is the provision that Presidents cannot pass laws without the approval of Congress. The English Bill of Rights also provided protection to citizens against "cruel and unusual punishment" and "excessive bail," both provisions also found in America; and it established the right of citizens to take up grievances with the government, also a right in America.

9. B: The correct answer is "A new political party and movement achieved greater success in several provinces." This answer describes how the CCF (and later the NDP), and the labour

movement more generally, had a long and continuing role in Canadian society. The city of Winnipeg has a real police force, and British labour activists are no longer considered a threat in Canada, so neither of those answers are correct. Inflation can be a problem at times, but has not remained consistently high, so this answer is also false. Strikes are fairly common in Canada, although much smaller than the General Strike, so it would be inaccurate to state that they have become much less common long-term.

10. C: While choice A is a historical event, it is not a long-term consequence, as trade does currently exist between East and West. The Mongol Expansion did establish Mongolia as a key power, but this did not continue into the 20th century, so choice B cannot be correct. The War of the Heavenly Horses occurred between 104 and 101 BC, and was, at least in part, sparked by trade disputes, but this would not be considered a long-term consequence still impacting us today. Finally, choice E is also not correct, as trade between these empires would not be a direct long-term consequence still impacting the world today.

11. B: Preservatives such as salt were only introduced to the European diet after trade routes opened and these goods could be brought to Europe.

12. D: The Maratha Empire or Maratha Confederacy controlled a majority of India in the middle of the 18th century. In chronological order, the Maurya Empire (b) ruled India in the 3rd century B.C., prospering under the command of Ashoka the Great. The Gupta Dynasty (a) ruled India beginning in the 3rd century A.D. (i.e. 600 years after the Maurya Empire). The Gupta Dynasty presided over ancient India's "Golden Age." After a number of invasions coming from the steppes of central Asia between the 10th and 12th centuries, the Delhi Sultanate came to dominate a majority of northern India, circa 1206-1526. The Mughal Empire (c) ruled this area after the Delhi Sultanate, from 1526 to the middle of the 19th century.

13. C: The rainforest is endangered by unsustainable agricultural, ranching, mining, and logging practices. Scientific researchers, on the other hand, have generally been successful in studying the rich diversity of rainforest flora and fauna without damaging the ecosystem.

14. B: Carrie Chapman Catt (1859-1947) was serving her second term as president of the National American Woman Suffrage Association when the Nineteenth Amendment granted the vote to American women. Elected to the presidency in 1913, Wilson announced his support of women's suffrage in 1918. The National Woman's Party, which continues to function as an educational organization, was founded in 1917 to fight for the passage of a Constitutional amendment to guarantee women's suffrage. World War I ended in 1919.

15. B: In the Dred Scot case of 1857, the Supreme Court ruled that Dred Scott was not a citizen and had no right to bring his case to court.

16. B: The 95 Theses were part of a letter of protest that Martin Luther wrote to his archbishop in 1517, when Luther was a monk in the Catholic Church. These theses criticized church practices, particularly the practice of selling indulgences. Some sources claim Luther nailed this document to the door of the All Saint's Church in Wittenberg (located in modern-day Germany). Luther's intention was to reform the Catholic Church from within, but his letter soon placed him at the center of a religious and civil revolt. He was excommunicated in 1520.

17. B: The Shoguns were Japanese military leaders. During the Tokuwaga shogunate, which began in 1603, the shogun held the actual power in the Japanese government even though Japan was technically ruled by an emperor. In actuality, the emperor was primarily a ceremonial leader and access to him was restricted to members of the shogun's family.

18. A: The Supreme Court upheld affirmative action in *Bakke v. University of California,* is not true. In this 1978 case, the Supreme Court actually overturned the earlier affirmative action provision to use quotas for the purpose of attaining racial balance. It is true that when affirmative action began in the 1960s, its aim was to remedy underrepresentation of blacks in higher education and employment by raising the numbers of blacks included until they came closer to being balanced with the numbers of whites (B). Since then, whites opposing affirmative action criticized the ruling insisting that instead of producing the desired goal, affirmative action discriminated against white applicants by pressuring schools and companies to preferentially accept black applicants (C). After the *Bakke v. University of California* decision, additional Supreme Court rulings followed the precedent of that case and further limited what affirmative action could legally do (D).

19. D: It is not true that (D) General Douglas MacArthur's invasion of Inchon was unsuccessful. While previous US interventions did not succeed in Korea, MacArthur's attack at Inchon on September 15, 1950, forced North Korean troops to retreat behind the 38th parallel, the temporary division set up after the war, which the North Koreans had breached on June 25, 1950. The other answers are true.

20. D: It is not true that Colonel Nicols granted very few civil or political rights to New York colonials. In fact, he gave them as many civil and political rights as possible to make up for the fact that James, Duke of York, who conquered New Amsterdam with his brother King Charles II's authorization (B), was strongly against representation for colonists, and prohibited any representative assemblies in his renamed New York (C). Despite Nicols' allowing colonial citizens many other rights, they still wanted to govern themselves, especially Long Island's Puritans (E). James gave in to their demands in the 1680s, but upon his accession to the throne of England in 1685, he went back on his word. It is true that before the English conquered the New York territories, New Amsterdam on Manhattan Island was a trading settlement of the New Netherlands made by Dutch explorers to facilitate the Dutch West India Company's fur trade with the indigenous peoples (A).

21. B: The Scientific Revolution emphasized careful observation of the natural world and applied reason to make and test generalizations about how it operated. The Scientific Revolution saw its zenith in the wide-ranging discoveries of Sir Isaac Newton (1642-1727:.

22. D: The written works Thomas Paine published *after* the American Revolution (1765-1783) were both *Rights of Man* and *The Age of Reason*. His *Rights of Man* (B) was published in 1791 in response to Edmund Burke's pamphlet *Reflections on the Revolution in France*, which criticized the French Revolution. Paine's *Rights of Man* defended the French Revolution. *The Age of Reason* (C) was a book Paine published in 1793-1794, which advocated deism and rationalism while criticizing traditional Christian beliefs and institutionalized religions. *Common Sense* (A) was a pamphlet Paine published in 1776, which was widely read and very influential to the American Revolution. Paine also published a series of pro-revolutionary pamphlets from 1776-1783 entitled *The American Crisis*.

23. C: The original six members of the European Economic Community began reducing trade barriers among its members as early as 1957. By 1992, the twelve member states were ready to further merge their national economies. The Maastricht Treaty official created the European Union and laid the groundwork for acceptance of the euro as a common currency. Member states of the UN, NATO, and OPEC share many common interests but have not attempted comparable economic integration.

24. B: The Warsaw Treaty Organization was meant to counterbalance NATO, or the North Atlantic Treaty Organization. Members of NATO included the United States, Great Britain, France and West Germany and pledged to consider an attack on one of them as an attack on all of them. NAFTA (the North American Free Trade Agreement) was signed by President Clinton in 1994 and lifted most trade barriers between the United States, Mexico and, Canada. The Soviet Union was a member of the U.N. Security Counsel which is charged with maintaining international Peace and Security.

The Four Power Pact was a pre-World War II treaty in which the United States, Great Britain, Japan and France agreed to respect each other's Pacific territories.

25. C: The rates of both productivity and inflation in the US were approximately 2% by 2000. By this time, the US economy was not increasing at a rate of 5% a year (A) but of 4% a year. Almost half of industrial growth contributing to economic prosperity was due to the "information revolution" made possible by the invention of the PC. The rate of unemployment in America at this time had not gone down to 6% (B) but to 4.7%. The stock market in the US had not just doubled in six years (D); it had actually quadrupled from 1992-1998 due to the increase in American households that owned stocks or bonds. Most of this ownership resulted from tax law changes regulating retirement accounts.

26. D: Japan did not experience more war soon after WWII. Japan not only had good economic recovery from the war, as some other nations did, but it also experienced tremendous economic growth. Within 40 years of the war's end, Japan boasted one of the world's strongest economies. Greece (A) experienced a civil war from 1946-1949 between the government's army and the Communist Party's army. China (B) went back to the civil war it had been fighting on and off since 1927, resuming the fighting from 1946 until 1950. Korea (C) began the Korean War in 1950 when North Korea invaded South Korea.

27. D: After being re-elected in 1948, Truman continued to promote his "Fair Deal," but Southern members of Congress from both Democratic and Republican parties prevented most of the programs from passing into law. When Congress passed the Taft-Hartley Act in 1947, it was not with Truman's agreement (A); Congress passed this law after Truman vetoed it. The Taft-Hartley act did not allow workplace to restrict their employees to union members (B); this act outlawed such "closed shops," which mitigated the power of labor unions. Congress did not raise the amount of aid to farmers or pass bills for health insurance and minimum wages (C); conversely, Congress reduced financial support for farming and turned down bills to providing health insurance and establishing a minimum wage. In fact, Truman's reelection was somewhat unexpected because many Americans did not approve of Congress' actions (E). Most voters were displeased by Congress' limitation of labor unions, lack of support for farmers, refusal to enact provisions for health coverage, and its refusal to establish a minimum wage.

28. C: Pope Urban II's plan for an army made up of previously trained military personnel was thwarted by the popular excitement concerning the First Crusade. This led to the creation of large armies primarily made up of untrained, unskilled, undisciplined, and ill- or unequipped soldiers, most of whom were recruited from the poorest levels of society. These armies were the first to set forth on the Crusade, which became known as the People's Crusade. Even though some of these armies contained knights, they were ultimately ineffective as fighting forces. These armies were prone to rioting and raiding surrounding areas for food and supplies and were viewed as a destabilizing influence by local leaders. They were defeated in battle and many converted to Islam to avoid being killed.

29. D: Around 600 BC, the Lydians of Asia Minor were one of the first to coin metal currency.

30. A: The Dominion of Canada, or simply Canada, as it is now called, is a confederation of ten provinces and three territories. The process by which these provinces and territories joined is commonly called "confederation." Unification is a broader term referring to the process of bringing individual parts into a whole. Federalization is the process of uniting into a federal system, or bringing an agency under federal jurisdiction. Ratification is the process of giving formal assent to a treaty, contract or agreement. Decentralization is the process of transferring control from a central organization to local or regional organizations.

31. A: In the 17th century, the Dutch Republic was really a loose confederacy composed of states which had sovereignty. Holland was the strongest province in this Republic, but it did not centrally govern the other sovereign states and could not even control them. The Dutch did enjoy world power status economically and nautically during the 17th century (B). This ended in the 18th century when England and France overpowered the Dutch. The Dutch East India Company was formed for trading in Asia, and Dutch merchants settled and also traded in South Africa, as well as conducting trade in North America and the Caribbean at this time (C). Two hallmarks of this period in the Netherlands were religious tolerance, such that it became a haven for many Europeans who escaped religious persecution in their countries by moving there, and the Dutch Golden Age of art (D), exemplified by artists such as Rembrandt, Vermeer, Frans Hals, and Jacob van Ruisdael. During the 17th century, the city of Amsterdam was a world center for banking, and Hugo Grotius and other Dutch philosophers were proponents of international free trade (E).

32. A: There was not less immigration to the US from 2000-2005 than in other years. In fact, more immigration to the US occurred in these five years than in any other five-year period of US history (b). It is true that borders were more secure following the terrorist attacks of 9/11/2001 (c). However, despite increased security measures, almost eight million people immigrated to the US (d), and of these numbers, nearly half entered the country illegally.

33. E: The most correct identification of the source of the term "Indians" for Native Americans is: Columbus, while searching for a water route to Asia, stumbled upon the Americas but thought he had landed in the West Indies. As a result, he called the natives "Indians" and the name became a tradition. "Indian" is neither a translation of a tribal word (A) nor a variation of the word aborigine (B). "Aborigine" is a synonym with "indigenous" but is not related to the term "Indian" It does not refer to Native Americans having originally migrated from India (C); instead, the predominant theory asserts that they migrated from Eurasia. It is also not a synonym for "indigenous" (D).

34. B: The Communist Manifesto claims that history has been a series of class struggles; that the rise of Communism will eliminate class boundaries and end the struggle. Karl Marx, the Manifesto's primary author, ended with a call for the working class of the world to start a revolution against the order of things, forcibly taking over the means of production. The final lines read:

"The Communists disdain to conceal their views and aims. They openly declare that their ends can be attained only by the forcible overthrow of all existing social conditions. Let the ruling classes tremble at a Communist revolution. The proletarians have nothing to lose but their chains. They have a world to win. Workingmen of all countries, unite!"

35. D: This cartoonist depicts a smiling John A. MacDonald observing a Canadian farmer and a Canadian mechanic enjoying the profits resulting from the National Policy with American manufacturers left out, indicating that Canadian industry would benefit at the acceptable expense of American manufacturers. The image does not suggest that the Canadians in the image are doing something wrong, nor does the image indicate whether the cartoonist thinks that the policy will ultimately fail, nor does it appear to make any claims about trade deficits. The cartoonist also does not mention or suggest anything about Canadian manufacturing, nor does it suggest that Prime Minister MacDonald would personally benefit. The correct answer is that the National Policy would result in higher profits for Canadian farmers and mechanics, and that the only group to lose would be American manufacturers.

36. D: It is not true that cotton farming was the reason Southern colonies imported more slaves in the 1600s. Tobacco farming was the reason. Tobacco became a very successful cash crop at that time in the American colonies. Growing tobacco was extremely labor-intensive, so planters needed more laborers as tobacco became more popular and valuable. Cotton was grown in America by the end of the 16th century and increased around the end of the 18th century due to Eli Whitney's invention of the cotton gin in 1793. It is true that slaves were brought from Africa to Florida by the Spanish as early as the 1560s (A), although this practice became more widespread practice in the 1600s. Chattel slavery (meaning outright ownership of a person for that person's lifetime) was legal in America from 1654 until 1865 (B) when Lincoln's Emancipation Proclamation abolished it. Furthermore, indentured servants provided sources of labor in America before slaves (C). Early indentured servitude was not race based, as the modern concept of race did not begin until the 1700s. Indentured servants were people who were bonded into servitude for a period of several years, often as a result of poverty, after which they could gain their freedom. An eventual shortage of indentured servants led to the importation of slaves and the enslavement of some indentured servants of African descent. By the end of the 17th century, court rulings had confined American slavery to people of African descent.

37. D: It is not a fact that the Treaty of Westphalia provided for reparations to France, choice D, or even that France had undergone war damages. In fact, the majority of the Thirty Years' War was fought in central Europe, and none of it was fought in France at all, so this answer is untrue. It is a fact that this treaty gave political recognition to the independence of the countries that are now Switzerland, choice A and Holland, choice B. The Treaty of Westphalia also prepared the way for political secularization of Europe, choice C. In addition, this treaty marked the decrease in the Pope's influence over Europe: He stated he was against the treaty, but the signing parties paid no attention to his objections, choice E.

38. C: Problems of hostile groups that coexist in India (C) are not a consequence of the British Empire. Like America (A), Jamaica (B), and Hong Kong (E), India is a country which enjoys freedom as aftermath consequence of the former British Empire. Problems of hostile groups in African countries (D) are a result of the former British Empire and other countries (such as France and Portugal) that colonized in Africa as these European imperialists set artificial boundaries, creating nations within which hostile groups were forced to coexist even though their cultural traditions and customs were incompatible. As these boundaries remain, the problems within African countries have continued beyond the days of British rule.

39. D: Despite the growing amount of literacy in the 1500s, due principally to the invention of the printing press and the availability of texts, the majority of Europeans remained illiterate.

40. A: The latest occurring decolonization event was the Eastern Bloc and Soviet Satellite states of Armenia, Azerbaijan, Estonia, Georgia, Kazakhstan, Kyrgyzstan, Latvia, Lithuania, Moldova, Russia, Tajikistan, Turkmenistan, Ukraine, and Uzbekistan, which all became independent from the Soviet Union in 1991. (Note: This was the last decolonization of the Cold War years, as the end of the Soviet Union marked the end of the Cold War.) Canada completed its independence from British Parliament via the Canada Act in 1982. In the Caribbean, the Bahamas gained independence from the United Kingdom in 1973. Algeria won its independence from France when the Algerian War of Independence, begun in 1954, ended in 1962.

41. A: At the Battle of Saratoga, aided greatly by Benedict Arnold's leadership, the troops of American General Horatio Gates defeated British General John Burgoyne's troops at Saratoga, New York, on October 17, 1777. After witnessing this victory by the Americans, France entered the war against Britain to support the Americans. Earlier, at Brandywine Creek (B), on September 1, 1777, George Washington was unable to stop British General William Howe from advancing to occupy Philadelphia. A bit earlier still, at the Battle of Oriskany (C) on August 6, 1777, British troops and Iroquois Indians led by Colonel Barry St. Leger defeated and killed America's General Nicholas Herkimer, but then had to retreat to Canada. Following this, in the middle of August 1777, the New England militia, commanded by General John Stark, defeated one of British General Burgoyne's detachments near Bennington, Vermont (D). (Note: the Battle of Saratoga was the last battle to take place out of the choices presented.) Since (A) is correct, answer (E) is incorrect.

42. D: By 1950, the number of women in the workforce had climbed to 28.8%. This was the first time that the percentage was above 25%. Choice A is incorrect because women in 1900 made up only 18.1% of the workforce. By 1920, women still made up only 20.4% of the workforce. So, choice B is incorrect. In 1940, 24.3% of women were in the labor force, but the question asks for a percentage higher than 25.

43. B: The Mongol people have traditionally been nomads living in large white felt tents that are commonly known as "yurts" or "gers" and in Mongolia, many of these people still live in this traditional housing. The term yurt is of Turkish and Russian origins, while ger is the Mongolian term. The Mongol ger is designed, decorated and positioned based on a strict formula determined by religion, tradition, and superstition. Today the Mongol people are spread over the Asian steppe region including Mongolia, and parts of Russia, China Afghanistan and Pakistan.

44. A: It is not true that England's defeat of the Spanish Armada in 1588 ended their war with Spain. It did establish England's naval dominance and strengthened England's future colonization of the New World, but the actual war between England and Spain did not end until 1604. It is true that Henry VIII's desire to divorce Catherine of Aragon strengthened English expansionism (B). Catherine was Spanish, and Henry split from the Catholic Church because it prohibited divorce. Henry's rejection of his Spanish wife and his subsequent support of the Protestant movement angered King Philip II of Spain and destroyed the formerly close ties between the two countries. When Elizabeth became Queen of England, she supported the Reformation as a Protestant, which also contributed to English colonization (C). Sir Francis Drake, one of the best known English sea captains during this time period, would attack and plunder Spanish ships that had plundered Native Americans (D), adding to the enmity between Spain and England. Queen Elizabeth invested in Drake's voyages and gave him her support in claiming territories for England (E).

45. D: Kiev, is part of Russia. The other choices were separate Kingdoms in the Iberian Peninsula — the area known as Spain — until Ferdinand and Isabella began consolidating the regions in the late 15th Century.

46. B: Of the cultures listed, only the Hebrews worshipped one God. Egyptians, Sumerians, Babylonians, and Hittites all practiced polytheistic religions that worshipped a host of deities.

47. A: Russian involvement in World War I brought social tension in Russia to a head. Contributing factors included military defeats and civilian suffering. Prior to Russia entering the war, Russian factory workers could legally strike, but during the war, it was illegal for them to act collectively. This eliminates answer C. Protests continued during World War I, and the Russian government was overthrown in 1917. This eliminates answer D. Answer B can be rejected because World War I did not go well for the Russian Army; Nicholas III, therefore, had no successes upon which to capitalize.

48. E: While a major contributor to the automotive industry, John D. Rockefeller (E) was not specifically an inventor, developer, or manufacturer of engines and/or cars. He was an American industrialist and philanthropist who founded and owned the Standard Oil Company from 1870-1897. Rockefeller transformed the petroleum industry, and in so doing, his company profited so much that he was often regarded as the richest man in history. In his time, Rockefeller was the richest man in the world and also the first billionaire in America. German Karl Benz (A) is generally credited with being the first to obtain a patent on a gas-powered automobile and founded the Mercedes-Benz auto manufacturing company. German Gottlieb Daimler (D) is credited with inventing the first high-speed petroleum engine, the first motorcycle, and the first motorboat. He and his partner Wilhelm Maybach designed the "Grandfather Clock engine," developed many other internal combustion engines, and formed the Daimler Motoren Gesellschaft (Daimler Motor Company), which later merged with Karl Benz's motor company. Rudolf Diesel (C), also from Germany, invented the diesel engine in 1897. American Henry Ford (B), who founded the Ford Motor Company, was responsible for a great many inventions, including the Model T and Model A automobiles, as well as the idea of creating assembly lines for the mass production of cars. His innovations allowed the majority of average consumers to be able to buy cars by the early 20th century.

49. B: The Founding Fathers decided that because the colonies did not have the right to elect members of Parliament, Parliament should not pass laws for them. The Declaration of Independence recognized the British Empire's government as being headed by the King of England, under whom the various local parliaments and legislative bodies served to enact laws for the peoples whom they represented. By addressing their ills to the King, the Founding Fathers sought to prevent the appearance that they acknowledged the British Parliament in London as having any authority over the American colonies.

50. E: All of these were scandals associated with corruption during Grant's presidency. The Black Friday Scandal (A) involved two businessmen, Jim Fiske and Jay Gould, who concocted a scheme to corner the gold market. They recruited Grant's brother-in-law to tell Grant that it would benefit the farmers to stop sales of gold by the government. Not knowing any better, Grant agreed, and the resultant drastic bidding up of gold prices on "Black Friday" ruined a good many businessmen. In 1873, Congress voted for the President to receive a 100% increase in salary and for Congress to receive a 50% increase, both retroactive for two years. This "Salary Grab Act" (B) outraged the people. When the Democrats won the next congressional election, they repealed the act. The Whiskey Ring Fraud (C) was a conspiracy by whiskey distillers and Treasury Department officers to defraud the government out of a great deal of money obtained from the whiskey tax. President Grant's personal secretary was involved in this. Also, again not knowing any better, Grant had received gifts offered to him that were suspect. When the fraud was investigated, Grant tried to protect his secretary. W.W. Belknap, Secretary of War under Grant, took bribes (D) from dishonest agents who had a part in the Department of War's administration of Indian affairs. Belknap resigned to avoid being impeached when the fact that he had accepted bribes became known. Other scandals during the Grant administration included the Credit Mobilier Scandal and the Sanborn Contract Fraud.

51. C: It is not true that the English Civil Wars between 1641 and 1651 legalized Parliament's consent as a requirement for a monarch to rule England. These wars did establish this idea as a precedent, but the later Glorious Revolution of 1688 actually made it legal that a monarch could not rule without Parliamentary consent. The wars from 1641-1651 were all fought between Royalists who supported an absolute monarchy and Parliamentarians who supported the joint government of a parliamentary monarchy (A). Parliament was the victor (B) in 1651 at the Battle of Worcester.

As a result of this battle, King Charles I was executed, and King Charles II was exiled. In the first of these civil wars, from 1642-1646, and the second, from 1648-1649, supporters of King Charles I (D) fought against supporters of the Long Parliament. The third, from 1649-1651, involved supporters of King Charles II (e) fighting against supporters of the Rump Parliament.

52. A: All of these countries experienced their own Renaissances following the Italian Renaissance, which began in the cities of Florence and Siena and spread through Italy. From there the intellectual and cultural developments of the period spread to France (B) from the late 15th to early 17th century, to Germany (C) in the 15th and 16th centuries, to England (D) from the early 16th to early 17th century, and to Poland (E) from the late 15th to late 16th century, as well as to the Netherlands in the 16th century, in a movement often known as the Northern Renaissance. This name distinguishes it from the original Italian Renaissance.

53. E: Between 1800 and 1900, the population of the city of London increased by six and a half times (E), going from around 1 million to 6.5 million. It did not increase by only two and a half times (A), three and a half times (B), four and a half times (C), or even five and a half times (D). (Note that this question and answer are different from the previous question and answer, #74, which refers to how much of the entire country of England's population was living in all the cities in England combined. This question refers only to England's capital and biggest city, London, and how much its population grew during the century.)

54. D: Political corruption was not an immediate effect of the rapid urban growth during this time. The accelerated growth of cities in America did soon result in services being unable to keep up with that growth. The results of this included deficiencies in clean water delivery and garbage collection, causing poor sanitation. That poor sanitation led to outbreaks of cholera and typhus, as well as typhoid fever epidemics. Police and fire fighting services could not keep up with the population increases, and were often inadequate. With people moving to the cities at such a fast rate, there were also deficits in housing and public transportation.

55. A: The historical evidence shows that the initial workers on tobacco plantations in Virginia were primarily indentured servants who would eventually receive their freedom. The path to slavery in its later forms was gradual, beginning with slavery as a form of punishment for legal infractions. Massachusetts became the first colony to legalize slavery in 1641, followed by other states, including Virginia. This was followed by laws declaring that any children born to a slave mother would be slaves themselves in 1662 and a later decision that all persons who were not Christians in their "native country" would be slaves in 1705.

AP Practice Test #2

Refer to the following for question 1:

Indigenous Peoples are those whose ancestors lived in Canada long before the arrival of European explorers and settlers. This term refers to three distinct groups: First Nations, Inuit and Métis. Indigenous Peoples live in all parts of Canada and come from many distinct nations with their own languages, cultures, and ways of being. While First Nations, Inuit and Métis Peoples have their own nations within Canada, they have also had a very positive impact on the history of Canadian society, despite Canada's historical mistreatment of Indigenous Peoples. Many inventions were first developed by Indigenous Peoples in Canada, including willow bark (source of aspirin), petroleum jelly, spruce gum, cultivated corn, sun goggles, snowshoes, wild rice, lacrosse, canoes, maple syrup, lawn darts, and many others. It's even believed by some experts that US and Canadian federal governance structures were loosely based on the government of the Iroquois confederacy!

The term "French Canadians" includes Acadiens, Québécois, and other groups of Canadians in places like Manitoba and northern Ontario. Acadiens (or Acadians in English) are the descendants of French colonists who arrived in Acadie during the 17th and 18th centuries. Acadie (or the Acadian nation) includes much of New Brunswick, Prince Edward Island, and Nova Scotia, as well as parts of Quebec.

Québécois (or Quebecers) live in Quebec, the second largest province by population. Quebec is the home of the Québécois nation, which was founded by French colonists in the 1600s and 1700s. Quebec is legally recognized as a nation within Canada and has a distinct cultural and linguistic identity.

Early English-speaking settlers to Canada arrived from England, Wales, Scotland, and Ireland and formed a series of British colonies which later joined with Quebec to form the Dominion of Canada. Many of Canada's legal, cultural and political institutions were inherited from these early pioneers.

Canada has enjoyed frequent waves of new citizens from all over the world for its entire history, making it among the world's most ethnically, culturally and linguistically diverse countries. In fact, Canada has one of the largest immigrant populations in the world, with nearly 25% born in another country. This number rises to approximately 50% in Toronto, Canada's largest city. Immigrants are a valued part of Canada's highly diverse and multicultural society.

1. Which of the following, if available, would challenge the author's assertion that Canada is one of the most culturally and linguistically diverse countries in the world?
   a. Confirmation that another country is more diverse based on migration records
   b. Speculation that Canada is less diverse than global averages
   c. Evidence that Canada was more diverse in the past than it is now
   d. Speculation that Canada is not as diverse as the author believes
   e. Immigration statistics which reveal low levels of historical immigration

2. When President Warren Harding called for a "Return to Normalcy" in 1920, the BEST summary of what he meant would be...
   a. A return to the high employment rate that had dominated the US during World War I
   b. A return to peaceful times and a focus on domestic issues, as opposed to a focus on international war
   c. A return to a period of high immigration rates that were contributing to a diverse culture and growing economy in the US
   d. A return to finding more territories, such as Puerto Rico and Guam acquired during the Spanish-American War, for expanding US markets

3. Most of the region known in ancient times as Mesopotamia is located in which present-day nation?
   a. Iran
   b. Saudi Arabia
   c. Turkmenistan
   d. Iraq

4. Which of the following is NOT true regarding the Virginia Companies?
   a. One of these companies, the Virginia Company of Plymouth, made its base in North America.
   b. One of these companies, the Virginia Company of London, made its base in Massachusetts.
   c. One company had a charter to colonize America between the Hudson and Cape Fear rivers.
   d. One company had a charter to colonize America from the Potomac River to north Maine.

5. How would this picture be most appropriately used?

Credit: National Archives and Records Administration.
http://teachpol.tcnj.edu/amer_pol_hist/thumbnail297.html

   a. As an example of a Suffragist picket sign.
   b. As an example of American response to Versailles Treaty.
   c. As an example of early American use of Biblical allusions.
   d. As an example of an early American response to the German Nazi movement.

6. Why did Henry VIII's daughter, Mary Tudor, earn the nickname "Bloody Mary"?
   a. She violently drove the Moors from her country.
   b. She declared war against France.
   c. She persecuted members of the Anglican Church.
   d. She refused to grant the king a divorce.
   e. She persecuted Catholics.

7. Which of the following scientific contributions was not made by Arabic thinkers?
   a. The development of the Arabic numbering system.
   b. The development of algebra.
   c. Significant advances in trigonometry.
   d. The invention of the abacus.
   e. Advances in the use of decimals.

8. Which of the following statements is correct?
   a. The Social Security Act was created as a part of the First New Deal.
   b. The Social Security Act was part of the First and Second New Deals.
   c. The Social Security Act was not part of either New Deal.
   d. The Social Security Act was created as part of the Second New Deal.
   e. The Social Security Act was a New Deal program with minor impact.

9. In FDR's second New Deal, which program was not authorized by the Emergency Relief Appropriation Act?
   a. The Public Works Administration
   b. The Works Progress Administration
   c. The Resettlement Administration
   d. Rural Electrification Administration
   e. The National Youth Administration

10. Which of the following is incorrect regarding the Virginia Companies?
    a. One of these companies, the Virginia Company of Plymouth, made its base in North America.
    b. One of these companies, the Virginia Company of London, made its base in Massachusetts.
    c. One company had a charter to colonize America between the Hudson and Cape Fear rivers.
    d. One company had a charter to colonize America from the Potomac River to north Maine.
    e. The Virginia Companies were both joint-stock companies that raised funds by selling stock.

11. Which of the following statements is true regarding New Spain in the 1500s?
    a. New Spain had not yet developed any kind of class system.
    b. The Spanish originally imported Africans to use as slaves for labor.
    c. The *hacienda* system eventually gave way to the *encomienda* system.
    d. Conquistadores experienced shortages of labor in the New World.

12. Under feudalism, this term refers to a person who controlled a large landholding and gave parts of it away in exchange for loyalty and protection.
    a. Fief.
    b. Homage.
    c. Lord.
    d. Primogeniture.
    e. Vassal.

13. Among the following countries, which was a French colony until the 20th century?
    a. Canada
    b. Algeria
    c. Indonesia
    d. Mozambique
    e. South Africa

14. **The bubonic plague spread through Europe in which of the following ways?**
    a. It spread along rivers and through contaminated drinking water.
    b. It was carried by birds that migrated south during the winter.
    c. It spread along trade routes, carried by infected animals and people on ships.
    d. It was carried by travelers on religious pilgrimages.

15. **Among the countries where Napoleon III tried to expand France's control, which did he *not* actually colonize?**
    a. Asia
    b. Italy
    c. Africa
    d. Mexico.
    e. None of these

16. **As a consequence of the second Industrial Revolution, the population of Berlin increased by more than ___ times between 1800 and 1900.**
    a. Five and a half
    b. Ten and a half
    c. Fifteen and a half
    d. Twenty and a half
    e. Twenty-five and a half

17. **The legislative structure set forth in the US Constitution was determined by:**
    a. The Virginia Plan
    b. The New Jersey Plan
    c. The Connecticut Compromise
    d. The Plan of Charles Pinckney
    e. The Plan of Alexander Hamilton

18. **Which of the following held themselves to the code of chivalry?**
    a. Serfs.
    b. Archbishops.
    c. Troubadours.
    d. Vassals.
    e. Knights.

19. **During the Civil Rights era of the 1950s, which of the following events furthered the civil rights cause?**
    a. The Supreme Court's decision in *Brown v. Board of Education of Topeka*
    b. Governor Orval Faubus' actions relative to Little Rock High School
    c. Eisenhower's use of the 101st Airborne Division to protect students
    d. The city of Little Rock's actions with regard to its high schools in 1958-1959
    e. Both answer a. and c. furthered the cause of civil rights.

20. Which of the following statements is correct regarding the American economy in the 1920s?
    a. America's gross national product went up 40% from 1919 to 1929.
    b. Three-quarters of the houses and apartments in America had electricity by this time.
    c. The number of people who owned cars in America quadrupled at this time.
    d. Twelve million American households had radios by the end of this decade.
    e. All of these statements are correct about the 1920s American economy.

Refer to the following for question 21:

Province or Territory	Joined Confederation
Alberta	1905
British Columbia	1871
Manitoba	1870
New Brunswick	1867
Newfoundland	1949
Northwest Territories	1870
Nova Scotia	1867
Nunavut	1999
Ontario	1867
Prince Edward Island	1873
Quebec	1867
Saskatchewan	1905
Yukon	1898

21. Which conclusion can best be drawn from the table above regarding the process of Canadian Confederation?
    a. Canada has continued to change and evolve throughout its history.
    b. Nunavut was established without the consent of its population.
    c. Discussions for a Maritime Union resulted in Confederation.
    d. None of the territories joined Canada until the 20th century.
    e. Canada is an ever-changing confederation, with members entering and exiting at will.

22. During the 15th century, Johann Gutenberg invented a printing press with moveable type. How did his invention influence science?
    a. It did not influence science; the printing of Gutenberg Bibles directed public attention away from science and toward reforming the Catholic Church.
    b. It led to scientific advances throughout Europe by spreading scientific knowledge.
    c. It influenced scientific advancement in Germany only, where Gutenberg's press was based.
    d. It did not influence science; though texts with scientific knowledge were printed, distribution of these texts was limited.

23. When was the first American transcontinental railroad finished?
    a. 1862
    b. 1890
    c. 1869
    d. 1865
    e. 1880

24. Which scientist first proposed the heliocentric universe instead of a geocentric one?
 a. Galileo
 b. Ptolemy
 c. Copernicus
 d. Isaac Newton

Refer to the following for question 25:

> The period from 1400 to 1600 in early modern Europe is often referred to as the Renaissance period. Although the exact dates and the nature of this time period have been disputed by some historians, the Renaissance (or "rebirth") is said to bridge the Middle Ages and the early Modern Age. While the Renaissance was a Europe-wide event, especially in Western Europe, it is most closely associated with Italy, where it began in the 14th century and swept outward.
>
> The Renaissance marks a time when interest in classical philosophy, art, and literature had been renewed. In particular, classical philosophy had been almost entirely forgotten or ignored during the Middle Ages among the general population Renaissance-era scholars thought of the Middle Ages as a period of cultural decline in Europe, which they sought to revitalize. The Renaissance impacted society much more broadly, however, as its influence was felt in science, music, religion, politics, and nearly every other aspect of European societies.
>
> Some scholars today believe that the Renaissance should be considered a cultural movement, rather than a specific time period. Others also suggest that the Middle Ages was not as anti-intellectual as is sometimes believed. While scholars in the Middle Ages focused primarily on the study of natural sciences, philosophy and mathematics, Renaissance scholarship also focused heavily on cultural writings, and that is, perhaps, the biggest change that swept Europe during the Renaissance.

25. What evidence provided by the author would support the view that the Middle Ages were not as intellectually backward as is often believed?
 a. The Renaissance was more of a cultural movement than a specific time period.
 b. Scholars in the Middle Ages studied natural sciences, philosophy and mathematics.
 c. Scholars in the Middle Ages ignored classic texts.
 d. The Renaissance can be seen as the bridging period between the medieval period and the Early Modern Age.
 e. Renaissance scholars believed the Middle Ages to be a period of cultural decline.

26. The 15th Century produced many influential artists in Florence, Italy whose work shaped much of what would become recognized as Renaissance art. Which of the following was not an artist from Florence?
 a. Filippo Brunelleschi.
 b. Masaccio.
 c. Lorenzo Ghiberti.
 d. Sandro Botticelli.
 e. Erasmus.

27. A historian is researching daily life in your home town in the 1840s. What might he do to locate sources?
   a. Contact descendants of people who lived in your town to see if they have any records
   b. Go to your home town's court house to see if land or court records are available.
   c. Go to your home town's library to see if they have information about the town's history
   d. All of the above

28. Which of the following was a long term effect of the New Deal?
   a. The end of the Great Depression
   b. An increase in the role the federal government played in the US economy.
   c. Decreased price supports for US farmers
   d. All of the above

29. Which of the following factors affecting American leisure pursuits in the 1920s is incorrect?
   a. Americans spent more money than previous generations on leisure pursuits.
   b. Americans had more time for leisure activities than did previous generations.
   c. Due to the influx in car ownership, Americans were more mobile.
   d. Movie theater attendance doubled.

30. Which statement about factors related to the growth of the US economy between 1945 and 1970 is incorrect?
   a. The Baby Boom's greatly increased birth rates contributed to economic growth during this time.
   b. The reduction in military spending after World War II contributed to the stronger US economy.
   c. Government programs and growing affluence nearly quadrupled college enrollments in 20 years.
   d. Increased mobility and bigger families caused fast suburban expansion, especially in the Sunbelt.
   e. Infant deaths were reduced by a third and the lifespan increased by four years during this time period.

31. Which of the following statements is *not* true about the Quakers?
   a. The colonies of Pennsylvania and Delaware were originally established to provide Quakers with religious freedom.
   b. The Quakers, though pacifists regarding war, were also aggressively subversive of social institutions and classes.
   c. The Quakers, while religious, did not assign much significance to the Bible or most human institutions.
   d. The Quakers were one of several radical religious groups formed in England around the time of the English Civil War.
   e. William Penn, a Quaker, established Pennsylvania to provide religious freedom, but there was initially no representative assembly.

32. What is the main way the US government controls our money supply?
    a. Changes in interest rates
    b. Raising taxes
    c. Striving for high economic growth
    d. Regulating inflation

33. To what does the name of the War of Jenkins' Ear refer?
    a. A war between England and Spain in the West Indies
    b. A war fought over a strain of corn grown in the US
    c. A war fought by England and France about Austria
    d. A war in which England and Prussia fought against France and Austria.
    e. A war begun in the American Ohio Valley against the French

34. Arabic mathematics most contributed to the development of mathematics in the Western world by:
    a. Founding the mathematics of calculus
    b. Using negative numbers in mathematical equations
    c. Founding the mathematics of probability
    d. Making important advances in algebra

35. The first coin-based economy was established by which of the following people?
    a. Phoenicians
    b. Egyptians
    c. Hebrews
    d. Lydians

36. Which of the following factors did not contribute to Spain's decline as a global power in the 16th Century?
    a. England's defeat of the Spanish Armada in 1588.
    b. A failed invasion of France.
    c. A huge trade deficit.
    d. Invasions by Moors who overtook much of the region.
    e. The Reconquista, an attempt to drive all non-Catholics out of Spain, which effectively cost Spain all of their talents and innovations.

37. United States Secretary of State Henry Kissinger most influenced the course of the Cold War by:
    a. Helping to slow the United States-Soviet Union arms race
    b. Helping to establish a cease-fire in the Arab-Israeli War in 1973
    c. Leaving the Soviet Union out of US efforts to end the Vietnam War
    d. Ordering a bombing campaign in Laos and Cambodia

38. Which of the following is the best example of a factor resulting from Europe's Commercial Revolution that contributed to the 1700s' Industrial Revolution?
    a. The rediscovery of concrete
    b. New advances in making iron
    c. The steam engine's invention
    d. Increases in population growth

39. Consider the map below. Shaded areas indicate water use, with darker areas indicating heavier use. On the basis of the map, which of the following is the best inference regarding the areas where there is no shading?

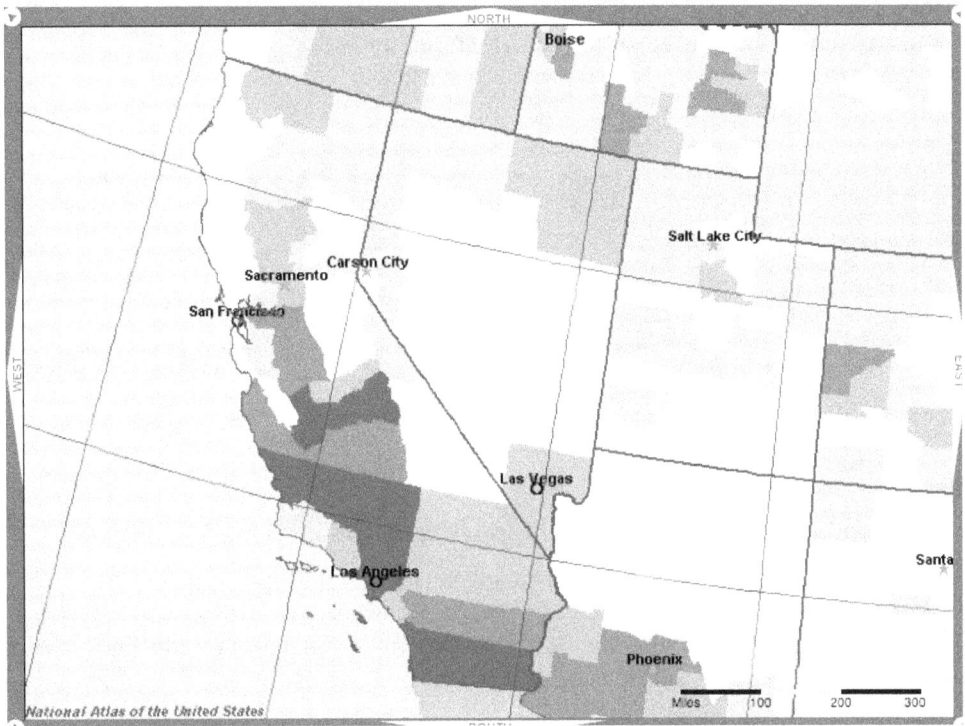

Map source: http://www.nationalatlas.gov/natlas/Natlasstart.asp

   a. They are less inhabited.
   b. They are more desert-like.
   c. Residents are better at conservation.
   d. Residents require less water per capita.

40. Which of the following American cities was not founded by people fleeing religious persecution?
   a. Plymouth, Massachusetts
   b. Jamestown, Virginia
   c. Boston, Massachusetts
   d. Providence, Rhode Island

41. Which of the following is NOT true about the Crusades?
   a. Their purpose was for European rulers to retake the Middle East from Muslims.
   b. The Crusades succeeded at European kings' goal of reclaiming the "holy land."
   c. The Crusades accelerated the already incipient decline of the Byzantine Empire.
   d. Egypt saw a return as a major Middle Eastern power as a result of the Crusades.

42. Which of the following is the most accurate description of the relationship between agriculture and industry in the 19th century?

a. With industrial and technological advances, farming was left behind in favor of industrial work.
b. With more urban workers needing food, farming became more important than industrial work.
c. Specialization and mechanization were applied more to agriculture at this time than to industry.
d. The development of both agriculture and industry was helped by technological innovations.

Refer to the following for question 43:

Native Civilizations in Central and South America

Civilization	Location	Conquered by	Date Empires Ended
Maya	Central America	Internal collapse	950
Aztec	Mexico	Spanish under Hernán Cortés	1519
Inca	Peru	Spanish under Francisco Pizarro	1533

43. Which of the following conclusions is supported by the information above?

a. Several nations in South America were conquered by Portugal.
b. The Aztec civilization was the oldest of the three listed.
c. Spain followed an aggressive policy of capturing new lands during the 16th century.
d. Incan warriors tried to assist the Aztec against the Spanish.

44. To what does the "long Parliament" refer?

a. A period when King James I clashed with Parliament because they denied his requests to raise taxes.
b. An eleven-year period when King Charles refused to allow Parliament to convene except when absolutely necessary.
c. Queen Elizabeth's reign, because she rarely called the Parliament into session.
d. A period when Parliament opposed English sea trade, which limited competition with other countries pursuing colonization.
e. The period when Parliament attempted to oppose the creation of the Anglican Church.

Refer to the following for question 45:

> Located on traditional Wabanaki Indigenous lands, Saint Croix Island is the location of an early attempt by the French to colonize North America in 1604. Late in the spring, Pierre Dugua, Sieur de Mons attempted to establish the first permanent French settlement in North America. The island had been used by the Peskotomuhkati as a location to store food, rather than a location suitable for habitation.
>
> At first, the island seemed ideal. Explorer Samuel de Champlain noted that the island was "covered with fir, birch, maple, and oak. It is naturally well located ... and is easy to fortify ... We considered this the best place we had seen on account of its location, fine surroundings and the interaction we were expecting with the Aboriginal peoples of these coasts and the interior, since we are in their midst ... Around our settlement at low tide there are plenty of shellfish—such as clams, mussels, sea-urchins, and snails ..."

Trade with the Peskotomuhkati (Passamaquoddy), Wolastoqey (Maliseet), and Mi'kmaw nations was exceptionally important to the new colony, as these nations could offer local knowledge of the territories and keep the colony supplied. By that winter, seventy-nine men were living on the island, including nobility, Catholic and Protestant clerics, doctors, workers, artisans, farmers, and soldiers.

That winter on the island was brutal, as the colonists were cut off from the mainland by ice and were covered by over a metre of snow from October to April. The island also had few trees, which meant little firewood and little protection from the wind. Access to fresh water and food was also limited. Many suffered from a disease now believed to be scurvy, and no remedy was available, so the suffering was very great. More than half died. The colony was abandoned, and the French tried again at a new location, Port-Royal in Nova Scotia, with more success.

In 1797, Robert Pagan of St. Andrews, New Brunswick proved that Dochet Island was the historic site of Saint Croix Island and the failed colony. The island was the location of a boundary dispute, with both the United States and Britain claiming the territory as their own. During the War of 1812, officials from the two powers would meet at Saint Croix Island, as it was considered neutral territory.

Today, a historical commemoration exists on both the US and Canadian sides of the Saint Croix River, which separates Maine from New Brunswick within the homelands of the Peskotomuhkati people, who continue to welcome visitors to the region.

45. What kinds of people were part of this first colony?
a. Labourers, nobility and Indigenous traders
b. Catholic priests, nuns and other clerics
c. Protestant priests and ministers, explorers, and royalty
d. A wide variety of people from all walks of life
e. Clerics, workers, doctors and nobility

46. The legislative structure set forth in the US Constitution was determined by:
a. The Virginia Plan
b. The New Jersey Plan
c. The Connecticut Compromise
d. The Plan of Charles Pinckney

47. What federal agency was NOT an outcome of World War I?
a. The Food Administration
b. The Fuel Administration
c. Railroad Administration
d. All of the above.
e. None were outcomes of World War I.

48. What did the Scientific Revolution emphasize?
   a. Tradition and authority.
   b. Observation and reason.
   c. Superstition.
   d. Theology.
   e. Mythology.

49. Which of the following statements is *not* true regarding the Huguenots?
   a. The policies of King Louis XIV caused many Huguenots to leave France.
   b. The Huguenots were French Catholics who were driven out by Protestants.
   c. Many Huguenots who left France settled in England, helping its economy.
   d. Many Huguenots who left France settled in Prussia, boosting its economy.
   e. Huguenots settling in the USA contributed to the ancestry of 11 presidents.

50. Which of the following is true regarding cotton production in Texas in the wake of the Civil War?
   a. Cotton production declined due to the loss of availability of slave labor to harvest the crops
   b. Cotton production declined due to the decrease in the demand for cotton across Europe
   c. Cotton production increased as Mexican and European immigrants took the place of slave labor
   d. Cotton production increased as an increase in the number of sharecroppers made harvesting more efficient

51. Which of the following is *not* true regarding the situation in the US before and around the presidential election of 1824?
   a. The majority of the states had removed property ownership as a prequalification for voting.
   b. Free black men did not have access to the polls in Southern states, but most voted in the North.
   c. The Massachusetts state constitution set a precedent in liberalizing voting requirements in 1820.
   d. Before 1824, there was little interest in national elections, as voters were left out of the process.
   e. In 1824, the legislative caucuses that previously made presidential nominations were not used.

52. A group that grew in numbers as a result of the Industrial Revolution was:
   a. Small farmers.
   b. Unskilled workers.
   c. Skilled craftsmen.
   d. The rural population.

Refer to the following for question 53:

> "As you know, I will soon be visiting the People's Republic of China and the Soviet Union. I go there with no illusions. We have great differences with both powers. We shall continue to have great differences. But peace depends on the ability of great powers to live together on the same planet despite their differences."

53. Which president gave this speech, as he was about to become the first US President to visit the communist People's Republic of China?
   a. President John F. Kennedy
   b. President Lyndon B. Johnson
   c. President Richard M. Nixon
   d. President Gerald R. Ford

54. The 1887 General Allotment Act, also known as the Dawes Act, had a policy of giving private property ownership to Native Americans in order to divide the Native American reservations into individual "family farms." What was a practical result of this policy?
   a. Many Native American tribes lost large portions of their reservations.
   b. Many Native Americans became assimilated to the American culture of family farming.
   c. The Nez Perce Conflict occurred between Nez Perce Native Americans and US army forces.
   d. American settlers moved to lands formerly owned by Native Americans and slaughtered most of the buffalo that Native Americans depended on for their livelihood.

55. Who was Lewis and Clark's guide?
   a. Pocahontas
   b. Sacagawea
   c. Squanto
   d. Wauwatosa

Answer Key and Explanations for Test #2

1. E: Immigration statistics would provide evidence affirming or challenging the author's claim that Canada is one of the most ethnically, culturally, and linguistically diverse countries in the world. Whether or not another country is more diverse would not impact this claim, as the author did not state that Canada is the most diverse, so choice A is incorrect. Choices B and D both involve speculation, so they would not be very compelling types of evidence. Choice C would also not be a good answer, as Canada's historical levels of diversity are not as relevant to the claim as the current levels. The correct answer references historical immigration, which would result (or not result) in current high levels of diversity.

2. B: It is the BEST summary for what President Warren Harding meant by a "Return to Normalcy." He was calling for a return to peaceful times and a focus on domestic issues, as opposed to a focus on international war. Choice A is a good guess because the president would want a good economy, and industry had been busy during WWI before falling off slightly after the war. But choice B is the best answer. He was not calling for going out in search of more territories or for higher immigration rates.

3. D: Lying between the Tigris and Euphrates rivers, the Mesopotamian region gave rise to many prominent cultures. Today, the land belongs mainly to Iraq while extending to parts of northeastern Syria, southeastern Turkey, and southwestern Iran.

4. B: The Virginia Company of London was based in London, not Massachusetts. It had a charter to colonize American land between the Hudson and Cape Fear rivers. The other Virginia Company was the Virginia Company of Plymouth, which was based in the American colony of Plymouth, Massachusetts. It had a charter to colonize North America between the Potomac River and the northern boundary of Maine. Both Virginia Companies were joint-stock companies, which had often been used by England for trading with other countries.

5. A: This picture was taken outside of the White House in 1918 and could be used to show students an example of a woman picketing as part of the fight to win the right to vote. In 1917, Alice Paul had begun organizing her followers into groups in order to picket the White House with signs intended to embarrass President Woodrow Wilson into supporting women's right to vote. These picketers did so at their own peril as many were arrested on charges of obstructing traffic. Those who were convicted served sentences at a local workhouse where they were subject to harsh conditions, including force-feedings.

6. C: A devout Catholic, Mary Tudor was known as "Bloody Mary" for her violent opposition to members of the Anglican Church, which her father, Henry VIII, created. She once burned 300 religious dissidents at the stake.

7. D: Each answer describes a significant contribution Arabic thinkers made to the sciences except D, the abacus, which predates Arabic culture.

8. D: The Social Security Act was created under FDR's Second New Deal in 1935. The Social Security Act was probably the most innovative, even revolutionary, reform measure of all of the New Deal programs in its provision of government-funded insurance benefits to citizens who are retired, unemployed, disabled, or dependent.

9. A: The Public Works Administration (A), or PWA, was not authorized under the Emergency Relief Appropriation Act of the Second New Deal. The PWA was created under the First New Deal by the National Industrial Recovery Act (NIRA), in 1933. Under the Second New Deal (1934-1935), the ERAA established the Works Progress Administration (B), which funded highway and bridge construction projects as well as countrywide cultural event. The ERAA also founded the Resettlement Administration (C) to help poor families in rural and urban areas relocate to government-planned communities.

The REA eventually became the Rural Utilities Service (RUS), which is a US Department of Agriculture (USDA) agency that still operates today.

The National Youth Administration (E) designed work-study programs for minors in relief families so that they could live at home, work part-time jobs and receive job training.

10. B: The Virginia Company of London was based in London, not Massachusetts. It had a charter to colonize American land between the Hudson and Cape Fear rivers (C). The other Virginia Company was the Virginia Company of Plymouth, which was based in the American colony of Plymouth, Massachusetts (A). It had a charter to colonize North America between the Potomac River and the northern boundary of Maine (D). Both Virginia Companies were joint-stock companies (E), which had often been used by England for trading with other countries.

11. D: The conquistadores had to deal with labor shortages during their colonization of America in the 16th century. To address the shortage of labor, the Spanish first used Indian slaves. Only after the Indians were decimated by diseases brought from Europe and from being overworked did the Spanish begin to import slaves from Africa (B). The first system used by the Spanish was the *encomienda* system of large estates or manors, which was only later succeeded by the *hacienda* system (C), which was similar but not as harsh. It is not true that New Spain's society had no kind of class system (A). In fact, this society was rigidly divided into three strata. The highest class was Spanish natives (*peninsulares*), the middle class consisted of those born in America to Spanish parents (*creoles*), and the lowest class was made up of Mestizos, or Indians.

12. C: Fief refers to the section of land a lord might grant. Homage refers to the oath of loyalty the recipient of the land would make to the lord. Primogeniture refers to the system of inheritance that granted the son of a lord complete ownership and control of his landholdings. Vassal is the person who would receive land from the lord.

13. B: Algeria was a French colony until the 20th century. Canada (A) was a British colony. (France did some colonizing in Canada, as is still evidenced by the use of the French language in part of the province of Québec, but all of Canada was made British property by the 1763 Treaty of Paris.) Indonesia (C) was a Dutch colony. Mozambique (D) was a Portuguese colony, and South Africa (E) was a British colony.

14. C: The bubonic plague spread along trade routes, carried by infected animals and people on ships. After reaching Cyprus in 1347, the epidemic followed trade routes to infect the populations of Italy and France. Then, also through trade routes, it traveled north to Germany, England, and eventually Scandinavia and Russia in 1351.

15. B: The country Napoleon III never actually colonized was Italy (B). He did promise the prime minister of Piedmont-Sardinia in 1858 that he would help Venetia and Lombardy, Italian provinces, to gain independence from the Austro-Hungarian Empire. However, Napoleon had his troops retreat from the fighting before the Italian provinces could be freed. In Asia (A) and Africa (C), France did succeed in colonizing some areas, and it kept these colonies until the middle of the 20th century. In Mexico (D), Napoleon III won a war and captured Mexico City in 1864, placing Prince Maximilian in charge. However, America was displeased with France's occupation of Mexico, and after the Civil War in America, Napoleon III was afraid of war with the United States and removed his forces from Mexico in 1867. Since (B) is correct, (E), none of these was never colonized by France, is incorrect.

16. C: As a consequence of the second Industrial Revolution, the population of Berlin increased between 1800 and 1900 by more than fifteen and a half times (C). In 1800, the population of Germany's capital and biggest city was around 172,000. By 1900, it had grown to 2.7 million. This equals 15.6976…times, or rounded up, 15.70 times—more than 15 and a half times its size a century earlier. Therefore, this city's population did not increase by only five and a half times (A) or ten and a half times (B). However, it also did not grow by as much as twenty and a half (D) or twenty-five and a half times (E).

17. C: The Connecticut Compromise was the plan that finally determined how the states would be represented in the government. During the Constitutional Convention or Philadelphia Convention, delegates drafting the Constitution disagreed on this point. The Virginia Plan (A), proposed by the Virginia delegation based on James Madison's ideas, held that states should be represented in proportion to their population sizes. Accordingly, the Virginia Plan was called the "large states plan." William Paterson proposed the New Jersey Plan (B). The New Jersey delegation objected to the Virginia Plan, as proportional representation could give unfair advantages to bigger states like Virginia and crowd out smaller states like New Jersey. The New Jersey Plan was called the "small states plan." It was rejected by the convention but helped small states have their point heard. The Plan of Charles Pinckney (D) of South Carolina has fewer recorded details as Pinckney did not present a written copy, and only James Madison's notes about it remain. The Convention did not debate Pinckney's plan. Alexander Hamilton's Plan (e) specified a strongly centralized government so similar to the British government that it was called the "British Plan." While delegates found Hamilton's plan well constructed, they rejected it for its similarity to Britain's structure, especially as Hamilton favored consolidating the states and the individual states opposed losing authority. The Connecticut Compromise (C), proposed by Robert Sherman, reached a balance between large and small states by stipulating the House would be represented in proportion to the states' populations while the Senate would have one vote per state. This combined elements of both the Virginia/large states and New Jersey/small states plans. It took delegates 42 days to agree to this conclusion, but the Connecticut Compromise finally resolved the issue of state representation.

18. E: The practice of chivalry refers to a code of conduct among knights. Serfs were peasants who worked the land and gave the crops to the lord, keeping enough for their own sustenance. Archbishops were members of the Roman Catholic church hierarchy. Troubadours were travelling musicians whose songs about chivalry kept the code alive in the popular imagination. Vassals were nobles who received land from lords in compensation for their loyalty and protection.

19. E: Both answer (A) and answer (C) furthered the civil rights cause, but (B) and (D) impeded this cause. In the case of *Brown v. Board of Education of Topeka* (A), the Supreme Court's 1954 ruling stated that schools segregated by race are by nature not equal. This ruling was monumental in the NAACP's fight against school segregation. Orval Faubus, Governor of Arkansas, tried to prevent Little Rock High School's integration in 1957 (B). The situation escalated to the point that President Eisenhower nationalized the Arkansas National Guard and sent the 101st Airborne Division to protect the high school students from harm (C). These actions furthered civil rights by showing the government's defense of school integration. The city of Little Rock, Arkansas and its high schools violated civil rights during that time period (D) and closed the high schools to prevent integration.

20. A: From 1919 to 1929, America's GNP rose by 40%. By the 1920s, only two-thirds of American households had electricity (B). The number of car owners did not quadruple at this time (C); however, it nearly tripled over the decade, from 8 million to 23 million. American households with radios did not reach 12 million by the end of the decade (D), but more than 10 million households did acquire radios by the end of the 1920s. Since only answer (A) is correct, answer (E) is incorrect.

21. A: The correct answer is "Canada has continued to change and evolve throughout its history." Several votes were held regarding Nunavut separating from the Northwest Territories to form its own, Inuit-led government beginning in 1982, and the territory was formed after much consultation and negotiation, so that answer is not correct. While the idea of the Maritime Union is older than Canada itself, these discussions have not yet been successful. Two of the three territories became members of Canada prior to the 20th century, so that answer also is not correct. While several provinces (most notably Quebec) have considered separating from Canada over its history, none have done so yet.

22. B: Johann Gutenberg's printing press led to increased scientific knowledge and advancement as scientific texts were printed and dispersed throughout Europe. Because the distribution of such texts extended outside of Germany, options C and D may be eliminated. Gutenberg Bibles were printed using Gutenberg's press, and thus Gutenberg's invention was likely a factor in the Reformation of the Catholic Church. In fact, Martin Luther's Ninety-Five Theses (against the Catholic Church) were printed using a printing press. However, this reformation occurred alongside, rather than in place of, the advancement of scientific knowledge. This eliminates option A.

23. C: The first transcontinental railroad was finished in 1869 (C) on May 10. Construction on the railroad was begun in 1862 (A) but not completed until seven years later. After completion, economic depression prevented more railroad building until the 1880s (E) and 1890s (B). In 1865 (D), there were 35 000 miles of railroad track in the country; by 1890 (B), there were 200 000 miles. The first transcontinental railroad connected the Central Pacific Railroad, which began in Sacramento, California, to the Union Pacific Railroad, which began in Omaha, Nebraska, in Utah.

24. C: Copernicus's *De Revolutionibus Orbium Coelestium (On the Revolutions of the Heavenly Spheres)* was published in 1543, almost simultaneously with his death. He was the first to contradict the then-accepted belief that the Earth was the center of the universe and the Sun and other bodies moved around it. This geocentric model was associated with Ptolemy and hence called the Ptolemaic system. Galileo Galilei published Siderius Nuncius (Starry Messenger) in 1610. In it, he revealed his observations, made through his improvements to the telescope, which corroborated Copernicus's theory. Sir Isaac Newton (1642–1727) built the first usable reflecting telescope and erased any lingering doubts about a heliocentric universe by describing universal gravitation and showing its congruence with Kepler's laws of planetary motion.

25. B: The text states that scholars in the Middle Ages continued to study natural sciences, philosophy and mathematics, although the common perception is that the Middle Ages completely lost all classical knowledge. Choice A may be factually true, but it does not support the view that the Middle Ages were not as "backward" as is often believed. Choice C is false, as this statement from the text would challenge the argument the author provides, rather than supporting it. Both choices D and E are true, but are not arguments in support of the author's statement.

26. E: Brunelleschi was an architect whose most famous construction is the Duomo in Florence. Masaccio was a painter whose frescoes demonstrate an early attempt to develop perspective that would later give Renaissance paintings their striking realism. Lorenzo Ghiberti was a sculptor noted for his "Gates of Paradise," the doors of the cathedral in Florence, adorned with sculptures depicting biblical scenes. Botticelli was a noted painter whose works include *Primavera* and *Birth of Venus*.

27. D: All of the listed methods are ways that a historian might locate sources, depending on his actual research question.

28. B: The New Deal did not end the Depression. The Depression only ended after the beginning of World War II when there was a huge increase in demand for goods and manpower. The New Deal increased the agricultural price supports offered to farmers and increased the role that the federal government played in the US economy.

29. D: During the 1920s, Americans *more than* doubled their attendance to movie theaters, with 40 million going to movies in 1922 and 100 million attending in 1930. The other statements are correct.

30. B: There was not a reduction in military spending after the war. Although the manufacturing demand for war supplies and the size of the military decreased, the government had increased military spending from $10 billion in 1947 to more than $50 billion by 1953—a more than fivefold increase. This increase strengthened the American economy. Other factors contributing to the strengthened economy included the significantly higher birth rates during the Baby Boom (A) from 1946 to 1957, which stimulated the growth of the building and automotive industries by increased demand. Government programs, such as the GI Bill (the Servicemen's Readjustment Act of 1944), other veterans' benefits, and the National Defense Education Act all encouraged college enrollments, which increased by nearly four times (C). Additionally, larger families, increased mobility and low-interest loans offered to veterans led to suburban development and growth (D) as well as an increased home construction. Improvements in public health were also results of the new affluence; the rate of infant deaths decreased significantly, and as a result, from 1946-1957, the American life span rose from 67 to 71 years (E). Moreover, Dr. Jonas Salk developed the polio vaccine in 1955, which virtually wiped out poliomyelitis, preventing many deaths and disabilities in children.

31. E: It is not true that Penn initially established his colony without representative assembly. He began the settlement by guaranteeing colonists not only complete religious freedom, but also a representative assembly. It is true that Pennsylvania and Delaware, which was originally part of Pennsylvania, were established to give Quakers religious freedom (A), which they did not enjoy anywhere else in Britain or America. In addition to being pacifists, it is true that the Quakers were aggressively outspoken against the establishment and the class system (B). The Quakers were religious, but their religious beliefs were that each individual could communicate directly with God, so they did not find either the Bible or most human institutions important (C). The Quakers did originate in England around the time of the English Civil War as one of several radical religious groups (D).

32. A: The Federal Reserve System raises and lowers the prime rate to regulate the nation's money supply.

33. A: The War of Jenkins' Ear was a war between England and Spain which started in 1739 when British Prime Minister Walpole conceded to Parliament's demands and sent troops to the West Indies, as well as to Gibraltar. Its name came from the fact that in 1731, a Spanish privateer cut off the ear of Robert Jenkins, captain of an English merchant vessel. Jenkins is said to have presented his severed ear to Parliament, adding to anti-Spanish sentiment in Britain and, along with other incidents, contributing to war with Spain. Thus Jenkins' "ear" does not refer to an ear of corn (B). The following year (1740), the War of Jenkins' Ear merged with the War of Austrian Succession, which was a war fought by England and France about Austria (C). France supported Prussia's actions against Austria, which was historically France's enemy. England wanted Austria to continue to control the Netherlands rather than for France to take over the Netherlands. These factors led to war between England and France. Within four years the conflict came to include American territory when the French backed Spain in the war against England. The War of Austrian Succession was concluded by the 1748 Treaty of Aix-la-Chapelle. In the Seven Years' War (1756-1763), Prussia allied with Britain and Austria allied with France against each other (D). Concurrently with the Seven Years' War in Europe, the French and Indian War (1754-1763) began in America when George Washington's troops fired on French troops in the Ohio Valley (E). In both Europe and America, the fighting ended with the 1763 Treaty of Paris.

34. D: Arabic mathematicians, such as the ninth-century mathematician al-Khwarizmi, made important contributions to algebra; the term "algebra" itself derives from a work of al-Khwarizmi's. However, Arabic algebra did not recognize negative numbers; this eliminates option B. Option C can be rejected because probability was developed initially by French mathematicians Blaise Pascal and Pierre de Fermat. Option A can be rejected because modern calculus (building on earlier foundations) is usually taken to have begun (separately) in the works of Isaac Newton and Gottfried Leibniz.

35. D: Around 600 BC, the Lydians of Asia Minor were one of the first to coin metal currency.

36. D: The Moors invaded Spain in the 700s. Although Spain's decline in power began to accelerate after the defeat of the Spanish Armada, many causes led up to the decline.

37. A: Henry Kissinger, US Secretary of State from 1973-1977 and National Security Adviser from 1969-1965, helped negotiate two agreements related to the arms race between the United States and the Soviet Union. According to one such agreement, SALT I (from the Strategic Arms Limitation Talks), the US and Soviet Union agreed to limit the number of offensive strategic missiles. Kissinger also helped to establish a cease-fire in the Arab-Israeli War in 1973, and he was also involved in a bombing campaign in Laos and Cambodia. However, neither of these events influenced the course of the Cold War to the degree to which the arms agreements did. Answers B and D respectively may thus be eliminated. Answer C can be rejected because Kissinger did attempt to involve the Soviet Union in US efforts to end the Vietnam War.

38. D: Increases in population growth supplied additional labor forces, helping to enable the Industrial Revolution. These increases were due to the prosperity brought through Europe's Commercial Revolution, which preceded the Industrial Revolution. The rediscovery of concrete, new advances in iron making, and the invention of the steam engine are all examples of developments that occurred during the Industrial Revolution.

39. A: The most reasonable inference based on the data given by the map is that the areas with no shading (which represent areas of low water use) are less inhabited than areas with shading. Note that the areas with no shading also have no listed cities; cities on the map are surrounded by shaded areas. Because the map does not give any information regarding how much water is required per capita, option D can be rejected. The map gives no indication regarding residents' prowess at conservation efforts (positive or negative). This eliminates option C. Additionally, there is no indication from the map that any land is more desert-like. In fact, some of the lightly-shaded area is adjacent to the ocean. Therefore, option B can be rejected.

40. B: Jamestown, Virginia was originally founded and settled by members of the Virginia Company of London, chartered by King James I of England. The Virginia Company was a profit-making venture and the first settlers of Jamestown were instructed to search for gold and a water route to Asia. Plymouth, Massachusetts was founded by the Pilgrims in 1620. Boston, Massachusetts was founded by the Puritans in 1630. The Pilgrims and Puritans were fleeing religious persecution in England. Providence, Rhode Island was founded in 1638 by followers of Roger Williams, a former Puritan leader, and his followers who had been exiled from Massachusetts due to their break with the Puritans.

41. B: It is not true that the Crusades succeeded at Christians' reclaiming the "holy land" (the Middle East) from Muslims. Despite their number (nine not counting the Northern Crusades) and longevity (1095-1291 not counting later similar campaigns), the Crusades never accomplished this purpose. While they did not take back the Middle East, the Crusades did succeed in exacerbating the decline of the Byzantine Empire, which lost more and more territory to the Ottoman Turks during this period. In addition, the Crusades resulted in Egypt's rise once again to become a major power of the Middle East as it had been in the past.

42. D: Advances in technology were applied not only to industrial production, but also to farming machinery. Farmers could then supply larger amounts of food to urban workers at lower prices. Farming was not abandoned in favor of industry (A). The many additional workers in cities needed food that they did not grow, so there was an even greater market for farming. This did not mean that farming took precedence over industry (B). Both fields increased during the 19th century, and they complemented one another. Specialization and mechanization were processes applied to both farming and industry. At this time, they were not applied more to farming (C) or industry.

43. C: The Spanish conquistadors were active in both Central and South America during the 16th century. Answer A is incorrect; Portugal was active in Brazil, but that location is not mentioned in the chart. The Mayan empire is older than both Aztec and Incan civilizations, making answer B incorrect. There is no indication that the Incan warriors in Peru tried to assist the Aztecs in Mexico when they battled the Spanish more than a decade before another conquistador would arrive in Peru.

44. B: The Long Parliament refers to the reign of Charles I whose attempts to raise taxes were repeatedly thwarted by Parliament. In response, Charles refused to allow Parliament to convene for eleven years and attempted to rule England as an absolute monarchy. In 1640, when Charles convened Parliament to help settle a Scottish uprising, Parliament passed laws limiting his power to convene and disband Parliament.

45. E: The text mentions that both Protestant and Catholic clerics were present, along with workers, doctors, nobility and people of other backgrounds. The colony did not include any Indigenous people, so choice A is false. The colony also did not include any women or children (the text mentions only "seventy-nine men"), so choices B and D are not correct. Choice C is also false, as there were no royalty present, and there were Catholics in addition to Protestant clerics.

46. C: The Connecticut Compromise was the plan that finally determined how the states would be represented in the government. During the Constitutional Convention or Philadelphia Convention, delegates drafting the Constitution disagreed on this point. The Virginia Plan (A), proposed by the Virginia delegation based on James Madison's ideas, held that states should be represented in proportion to their population sizes. Accordingly, the Virginia Plan was called the "large states plan." William Paterson proposed the New Jersey Plan (B). The New Jersey delegation objected to the Virginia Plan, as proportional representation could give unfair advantages to bigger states like

Virginia and crowd out smaller states like New Jersey. The New Jersey Plan was called the "small states plan." It was rejected by the convention but helped small states have their point heard. The Plan of Charles Pinckney (D) of South Carolina has fewer recorded details as Pinckney did not present a written copy, and only James Madison's notes about it remain. The Convention did not debate Pinckney's plan. The Connecticut Compromise (C), proposed by Robert Sherman, reached a balance between large and small states by stipulating the House of Representatives numbers would be in proportion to the states' populations while each state would have equal representation in the Senate, with two Senators. This combined elements of both the Virginia/large states and New Jersey/small states plans. It took delegates 42 days to agree to this conclusion, but the Connecticut Compromise finally resolved the issue of state representation.

47. D: All of the agencies listed (D) were federal agencies formed in response to World War I, and the institution of said agencies expanded the American federal government. The Food Administration (A) oversaw distribution and pricing of food. The Fuel Administration (B) managed distribution, pricing, and use of fuel for transportation. The Railroad Administration (C) worked with issues of railway transportation. Additional federal agencies included the War Industries Board, the War Shipping Board, and the National War Labor Board.

48. B: The Scientific Revolution emphasized careful observation of the natural world and applied reason to make and test generalizations about how it operated. The Scientific Revolution saw its zenith in the wide-ranging discoveries of Sir Isaac Newton (1642-1727).

49. B: The statement that is not true regarding the Huguenots is (B). The Huguenots were French Protestants, not Catholics, and they were driven out by Catholics, not Protestants. This was largely due to the policies of King Louis XIV (A). In 1685, he revoked the 1598 Edict of Nantes, which had provided for a modicum of religious toleration. Thereafter, Louis XIV effectively pushed many Huguenots out of the country. In retrospect, historians find that because the Huguenots were very hard workers and possessed many important skills, this excision of them was detrimental to France. Thousands of fleeing Huguenots settled in England, with their work in watchmaking and other industries strengthened England's economy (C). Fewer, but still thousands, of Huguenots settled in Prussia (then the territory of Brandenburg-Prussia) at ruler Frederick William's invitation, where they also contributed to the economy with their industrious habits (D). In addition, many Huguenots migrated to America, making significant contributions. In fact, there are 11 US presidents with Huguenots among their ancestors (E). These are: George Washington, John Quincy Adams, John Tyler, James Garfield, Theodore Roosevelt, William Howard Taft, Herbert Hoover, Franklin Delano Roosevelt, Harry S. Truman, George H.W. Bush, and George W. Bush.

50. C: Although Texas farmers lost slave labor after the civil war, cotton production actually increased in Texas from approximately 350,000 bales annually in the late 1860's to 3.5 million bales at the turn of the century. As cotton boomed in Texas, sharecroppers suffered from poor work and economic conditions. The primary beneficiaries of the cotton boom were landowners and the proprietors of large farms who benefited from a new influx of workers from Mexico and Europe.

51. B: Though it is true that free black men were not allowed to vote in the Southern states, it is not true that most of them voted in the North. In fact, in the majority of the Northern states, free black men were not allowed to vote, even in areas where they might have previously had this benefit without a formal amendment to the constitution. During the early part of the Jacksonian era, the trend was to exclude blacks politically, socially, and economically. It is true that by 1824, most states in the Union had gotten rid of the qualification stating that a person must own property in order to vote (A). The liberalization this change represented was inspired by the 1820 example of the state constitution of Massachusetts (C), the first to remove the property qualification. It is true that up until this election, there was little popular interest in national elections because legislative caucuses made presidential nominations, keeping voters uninvolved in such choices (D). It is also true that these caucuses were disregarded in 1824 (E) in favor of letting the people decide.

52. B: As production shifted to factories, a large number of unskilled workers were needed to operate the machinery that was beginning to put many skilled craftsmen out of work. As farms grew larger and increasingly mechanized, the number of people who owned their own farm began to decrease. The rural population declined as people flocked to the cities in search of employment.

53. C: The speech is from President Richard M. Nixon, who was about to become, in 1972, the first US president to visit the People's Republic of China. The other presidents listed are good guesses as they are from similar time periods and might have made similar speeches about China and the Soviet Union, but they are incorrect choices.

54. A: Choice D sounds like a good option, because this is something that did happen, but it happened before the Dawes Act. The Nez Perce conflict of 1877 also occurred before the Dawes Act, so choice C is incorrect. Choice B was the hope of Dawes and other American politicians who planned the act in order to try to help "assimilate" Native Americans, but that was not the practical result as much as choice A, the taking over of reservation lands away from Native Americans.

55. B: Sacagawea acted as Lewis and Clark's guide during their exploration of the Louisiana Purchase. She had been separated from her family at a young age and was reunited with her brother on the course of the expedition. Pocahontas was the daughter of Powhatan, the leader of the Algonquian tribes at the beginning of the 17th Century when the colony of Jamestown was founded in modern-day Virginia. Squanto's actual name was Tisquantum. He was the Native American who helped the Pilgrims after their first winter in Massachusetts. Wauwatosa is a suburb of Milwaukee, Wisconsin.

AP Practice Test #3

1. The catalyst to the onset of World War I was the assassination of Archduke Franz Ferdinand by
   a. Austrian terrorists.
   b. Russian nationalists.
   c. Serbian nationalists.
   d. German terrorists.
   e. French nationalists.

2. Who was Boris Yeltsin?
   a. A Russian politician credited with breaking up the USSR
   b. A Russian politician who was instrumental in the Russian Revolution
   c. A Ukrainian politician who encouraged his country to break away from the Eastern bloc countries
   d. A Scandinavian politician who successfully prevented his country from joining the Warsaw Pact

3. What would be the BEST title to summarize this list?
   - Poor agricultural practices
   - Years of drought
   - Lack of ground cover to hold soil in place
   - High winds on the plains

   a. Causes of the 1935 Dust Bowl
   b. Effects of the 1935 Dust Bowl
   c. Issues for the 1970s Era Rust Belt
   d. Issues for the 1970s Era Sun Belt

Refer to the following for question 4:

During a report on the Industrial Revolution, Mary uses a poster to illustrate cause and effect relationships in the War of 1812.

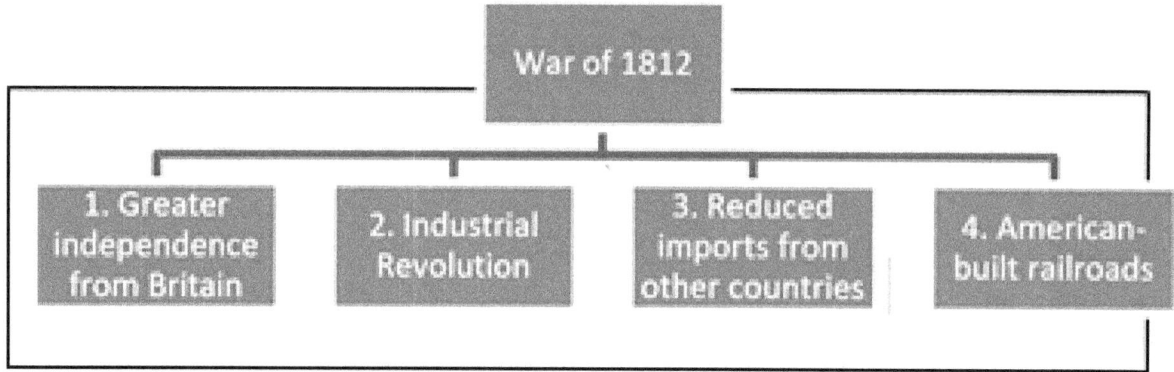

4. What could be added to make the organizer more informative?
   a. Placing boxes 1, 3 and 4 below box 2 and adding details to support
   b. A third tier that provides details about boxes 1, 2 and 3
   c. Handouts for each student to take home
   d. Music, video or other multimedia to make the presentation more interesting

5. Which of the following is NOT true regarding the Whiskey Rebellion?
   a. Washington's dispatching federal troops did not resolve the revolt, a setback for the government.
   b. An excise tax levied on whiskey was central to Treasury Secretary Hamilton's revenue program.
   c. Farmers in Pennsylvania objected to the excise tax on whiskey, and were refusing to pay the tax.
   d. Farmers in Pennsylvania committed acts of terrorism against tax collectors over the whiskey tax.
   e. President Washington sent a federal militia of 15,000 troops to address the Whiskey Rebellion.

6. Oklahoma became America's ___ state in ___.
   a. 40th; 1900
   b. 43rd; 1902
   c. 45th; 1905
   d. 46th; 1907

7. "Before his religious conversion, he persecuted Jews who converted to Christianity. After experiencing a religious vision, he became the early Christian church's strongest proponent, founding and counseling churches throughout Greece and Macedonia. These churches went on to form the foundation of the religion that would eventually spread throughout the Roman Empire."

The above passage describes which of the men below?

   a. Jesus
   b. Paul
   c. Peter
   d. David

8. Which of the following explorers was *not* involved in the search for a Northwest Passage?

   a. Verrazzano
   b. John Cabot
   c. Jacques Cartier
   d. Magellan
   e. All of the above explorers were involved in the search for a Northwest Passage.

9. Which western European monastic order developed an early form of banking that helped make pilgrimages to the Holy Land safer for the pilgrims?

   a. The Knights Templar
   b. The Knights Hospitaller
   c. The Knights of Malta
   d. The Barbary Corsairs

10. This medical scientist was the first to describe how blood cycles throughout the veins and heart.

    a. Francis Bacon.
    b. Roger Bacon.
    c. William Harvey.
    d. Ambroise Paré.
    e. Andreas Vesalius.

11. To what does the term "Black Death" refer?

    a. Viking warfare in the 9th Century.
    b. The plague that killed 25 million in the 1300s.
    c. An execution method common in the feudal system.
    d. Excommunication by the Catholic Church.
    e. A form of combat used among knights.

12. Which of the following was *not* a Southern reaction to the abolitionist movement?

    a. People defended slavery, citing scriptures as justifications.
    b. People cited "scientific" evidence of black "inferiority."
    c. Postal services charged extra to deliver anti-slavery mail.
    d. All disagreement was squelched, causing a closed society.
    e. Narrow mindedness made creative and academic writing wither.

13. What contributed to the weakening and collapse of the League of Nations?
   a. The failure of the United States to join
   b. The beginning of World War I
   c. The signing of the Treaty of Versailles
   d. The beginning of the Persian Wars

Refer to the following for question 14:

Located on traditional Wabanaki Indigenous lands, Saint Croix Island is the location of an early attempt by the French to colonize North America in 1604. Late in the spring, Pierre Dugua, Sieur de Mons attempted to establish the first permanent French settlement in North America. The island had been used by the Peskotomuhkati as a location to store food, rather than a location suitable for habitation.

At first, the island seemed ideal. Explorer Samuel de Champlain noted that the island was "covered with fir, birch, maple, and oak. It is naturally well located ... and is easy to fortify ... We considered this the best place we had seen on account of its location, fine surroundings and the interaction we were expecting with the Aboriginal peoples of these coasts and the interior, since we are in their midst ... Around our settlement at low tide there are plenty of shellfish—such as clams, mussels, sea-urchins, and snails ..."

Trade with the Peskotomuhkati (Passamaquoddy), Wolastoqey (Maliseet), and Mi'kmaw nations was exceptionally important to the new colony, as these nations could offer local knowledge of the territories and keep the colony supplied. By that winter, seventy-nine men were living on the island, including nobility, Catholic and Protestant clerics, doctors, workers, artisans, farmers, and soldiers.

That winter on the island was brutal, as the colonists were cut off from the mainland by ice and were covered by over a metre of snow from October to April. The island also had few trees, which meant little firewood and little protection from the wind. Access to fresh water and food was also limited. Many suffered from a disease now believed to be scurvy, and no remedy was available, so the suffering was very great. More than half died. The colony was abandoned, and the French tried again at a new location, Port-Royal in Nova Scotia, with more success.

In 1797, Robert Pagan of St. Andrews, New Brunswick proved that Dochet Island was the historic site of Saint Croix Island and the failed colony. The island was the location of a boundary dispute, with both the United States and Britain claiming the territory as their own. During the War of 1812, officials from the two powers would meet at Saint Croix Island, as it was considered neutral territory.

Today, a historical commemoration exists on both the US and Canadian sides of the Saint Croix River, which separates Maine from New Brunswick within the homelands of the Peskotomuhkati people, who continue to welcome visitors to the region.

14. Based on the passage, why does the author use the expression "a disease now believed to be scurvy"?
    a. It was originally believed that the colonists suffered from pellagra.
    b. The afflicted colonists died too quickly after falling ill for their symptoms to be recognized.
    c. Samuel de Champlain was likely not familiar with the disease and didn't refer to it as scurvy.
    d. Scurvy was a completely unknown disease until Vasco da Gama's voyages in 1497.
    e. The cause of scurvy was not well understood until James Lind's research in 1747.

15. A determinant of demand increases. What follows?

    I. The demand curve shifts to the right
    II. The equilibrium price increases
    III. The equilibrium quantity increases
    IV. The supply curve shifts to the left

    a. Only I
    b. I and II only
    c. I, II, and III only
    d. I, II, III, and IV

16. Of the following, which was not one of the first industries to develop in the western US?
    a. Gold mining
    b. Silver mining
    c. Lumber industry
    d. Cattle industry
    e. Sheepherding

17. Which of the following states was not one of the original seven to secede from the Union and form the Confederacy?
    a. South Carolina
    b. Georgia
    c. Texas
    d. North Carolina
    e. Florida

Refer to the following for question 18:

> "Efforts to build and sustain peace are necessary not only once conflict has broken out, but also long beforehand through preventing conflict and addressing its root causes. We must work better together across the peace continuum, focusing on all the dimensions of conflict." —UN Secretary-General António Guterres

Diplomatic Talks   Mediated Talks   Embargo   Sanction   Military Intervention

18. The United Nations has attempted to prevent war by using the methods on the continuum above. Which sequence of activities below would follow the continuum from more peaceful to less peaceful?
   a. Military intervention, embargo, diplomatic talks
   b. Sanction, embargo, military intervention
   c. Embargo, mediated talks, diplomatic talks
   d. Embargo, sanction, military intervention
   e. Diplomatic talks, sanction, mediated talks

19. Leonardo Da Vinci made important contributions to engineering, architecture, painting, sculpture, and science. Which of the following terms best describes him?
   a. Reformist.
   b. Renaissance Man.
   c. Humanist.
   d. Artist.
   e. Realist.

20. What was the purpose of the Mayflower Compact?
   a. To create and enact a series of laws for the Pilgrims.
   b. To create a temporary government for the Pilgrims.
   c. To memorialize the Pilgrims' promises to raise their children according to their religious ideals.
   d. To memorialize the laws under which the Pilgrims had previously been living

21. What statement would historians be least likely to agree with about Western civilization?
   a. By the beginning of the 21st century, Western civilization has not been as influential as others.
   b. The philosophical beliefs associated with communism have their origins in Western civilization.
   c. The philosophical beliefs associated with democracy have their origins in Western civilization.
   d. The great technological and educational advances in modern life are from Western civilization.
   e. One sign of great changes from 1648 to 2000 is that there was no such idea as a nation in 1648.

22. European colonization of present-day Pennsylvania in the late 17th century is most closely associated with:
   a. The desire for freedom of the press
   b. Escape from high taxes
   c. The desire for religious freedom
   d. Escape from trade restrictions

23. Who is the author of *Dialogue Concerning the Two Chief World Systems, Ptolemaic and Copernican* that argued the Earth was not the center of the universe?
    a. Copernicus.
    b. Galileo Galilei.
    c. Johannes Kepler.
    d. Rene Descartes.
    e. Francis Bacon.

24. In which of the following circumstances would it be appropriate to use a chronological view to understand history?
    a. When discussing the role of religion in ancient civilizations
    b. When discussing cultural differences between civilizations in different climates
    c. When discussing the US-Soviet race to the moon
    d. When looking at the role of families in various civilizations

25. Which of the following is not true of issues in America during the Clinton administration?
    a. Due to objections, Clinton amended his suspension of the ban on gays in the military to a "don't ask-don't tell" policy.
    b. The Family and Medical Leave Act was passed in 1993, reforming employee policies in the event of family emergencies.
    c. President Clinton proposed the provision of universal health care coverage, but it was rejected by Congress.
    d. Clinton's plan to remedy the federal deficit via raising taxes and reducing federal spending was passed by Congress.

26. Which of the following is *not* true regarding the British Empire?
    a. By the 20th century, the British Empire controlled over 25% of the world's population.
    b. The Rhodes Scholarships program is a legacy of the British Empire.
    c. African country Zimbabwe was formerly named after Cecil Rhodes.
    d. Great Britain is much smaller than the American state of California.
    e. All of these statements are true statements regarding the British Empire.

27. Which of the following laws was instrumental in spurring westward migration to the Great Plains between 1860 and 1880?
    a. The Homestead Act
    b. The Timber Culture Act
    c. The Desert Land Act
    d. All of these laws were instrumental in spurring westward migration to the Great Plains during that period.

28. Which of these is *not* true regarding the Second Industrial Revolution?
    a. The number of Germany's factories more than quadrupled during that time period.
    b. The United States and Germany were tied as leaders of industry during that time.
    c. The oil industry was one of the most significant components of industrial growth.
    d. The steel industry was one of the most important components of industrial growth.
    e. While big companies had previously existed, this was when modern "mega" businesses grew.

29. Who is the Italian writer whose book *The Prince* made his name synonymous with duplicity and dishonesty?
    a. Francesco Petrarch.
    b. Baldassare Castiglione.
    c. Filippo Brunelleschi.
    d. Sandro Botticelli.
    e. Niccolo Machiavelli.

30. Which conquistador discovered the Mississippi River?
    a. Coronado
    b. De Soto
    c. Cortes
    d. De Leon
    e. De Narvaez

31. Which of the following statements is correct regarding the Hapsburg Empire after 1648?
    a. The Hapsburg Empire shared postwar stability and homogeneity with Prussia.
    b. The Hapsburg Empire had military forces known for functioning smoothly after the war.
    c. Following the war, the Hapsburg Empire presided over a significant number of Muslims.
    d. After the war, the Hapsburg Empire included various languages and cultural groups.
    e. After the war, the Hapsburg Empire included various religious and political groups.

32. Which of the following rivers did NOT play an important role in the development of the earliest civilizations?
    a. The Tiber River
    b. The Yangtze River
    c. The Euphrates River
    d. The Nile River

33. Europe's Thirty Years' War was popularly known as
    a. a war of economy.
    b. a war of religion.
    c. a war of power.
    d. a war of commerce.
    e. a war of reform.

34. Which of the following statements is *incorrect* regarding the inception of the Georgia colony?
    a. Georgia was originally founded to create a buffer zone between South Carolina and Florida.
    b. British philanthropist General James Oglethorpe and his followers founded Georgia.
    c. The charter to establish a British colony in what is now Georgia was granted in 1765.
    d. Due to the founders' extensive rules, few settlers came, and those few were unhappy.
    e. Georgia's original settlers were British subjects who were economically unsuccessful.

35. Read the following passage:

Islam spread to Europe during the medieval period, bringing scientific and technological insights. The Muslim emphasis on knowledge and learning can be traced to an emphasis on both in the Qur'an [Koran], the holy book of Islam. Because of this emphasis, scholars preserved some of the Greek and Roman texts that were lost to the rest of Europe. The writings of Aristotle, among others, were saved by Muslim translators. Islamic scholars modified a Hindu number system, which became the more commonly used Arabic system, which replaced Roman numerals. They also developed algebra and invented the astrolabe, a device for telling time that also helped sailors to navigate. In medicine, Muslim doctors cleaned wounds with antiseptics, closed the wounds with gut and silk sutures, and were among the first to use sedatives.

Based on the information above, which of the following conclusions is likely true?
   a. People of Muslim faith were braver than others when facing surgery.
   b. Fewer Muslim patients died of wound infections than did their European counterparts.
   c. The silk market expanded because of the Muslim use of silk sutures.
   d. No one would read Aristotle today had the Muslims not saved the translations.

36. **Which of the following was not part of President Nixon's policy of "Vietnamization?"**
   a. The US contributed monetary assistance to the South Vietnamese.
   b. South Vietnam would be given more responsibility for the war in this policy.
   c. President Nixon began removing US troops from the country in increments.
   d. President Nixon accelerated the US bombing of North Vietnam in this policy.
   e. All of these things were elements of President Nixon's "Vietnamization" policy.

37. **Which of the following statements about the education of wealthy Athenian males is false?**
   a. Children attended group schools where they studied reading, writing, poetry, and grammar.
   b. Children were taken out of their homes and placed in a grueling public education program designed to build physical and psychological endurance.
   c. Children studied sports such as gymnastics, javelin throwing, and boxing.
   d. Adolescents studied government, ethics, mathematics, and rhetoric in the schools of the Sophists.
   e. Eighteen-year olds were obligated to spend one year in military service.

38. **Members of this wealthy family were famous for financing many great works by Italian artists in the 15th Century. They were known as patrons.**
   a. The Medici.
   b. The Machiavelli.
   c. The Ghiberti.
   d. The Brunischelli.
   e. The Botticelli.

39. Around the turn of the 19th and 20th century, when city slums resulted from overcrowding due to immigration, in which of the following areas was the least improvement made?
   a. Housing
   b. Sewage
   c. Firefighting
   d. Street lights
   e. Water supply

40. Which statement is *not* true regarding the years after the War of 1812 in America?
   a. America experienced accelerated economic and social development during this time.
   b. Overly rapid progress alternating with depression caused a negative popular mood.
   c. There was a severe depression in 1819, a backlash against accelerated growth.
   d. America was changing from an agricultural society into an industrial society.
   e. The trend toward westward expansion in the United States gained more momentum.

Refer to the following for question 41:

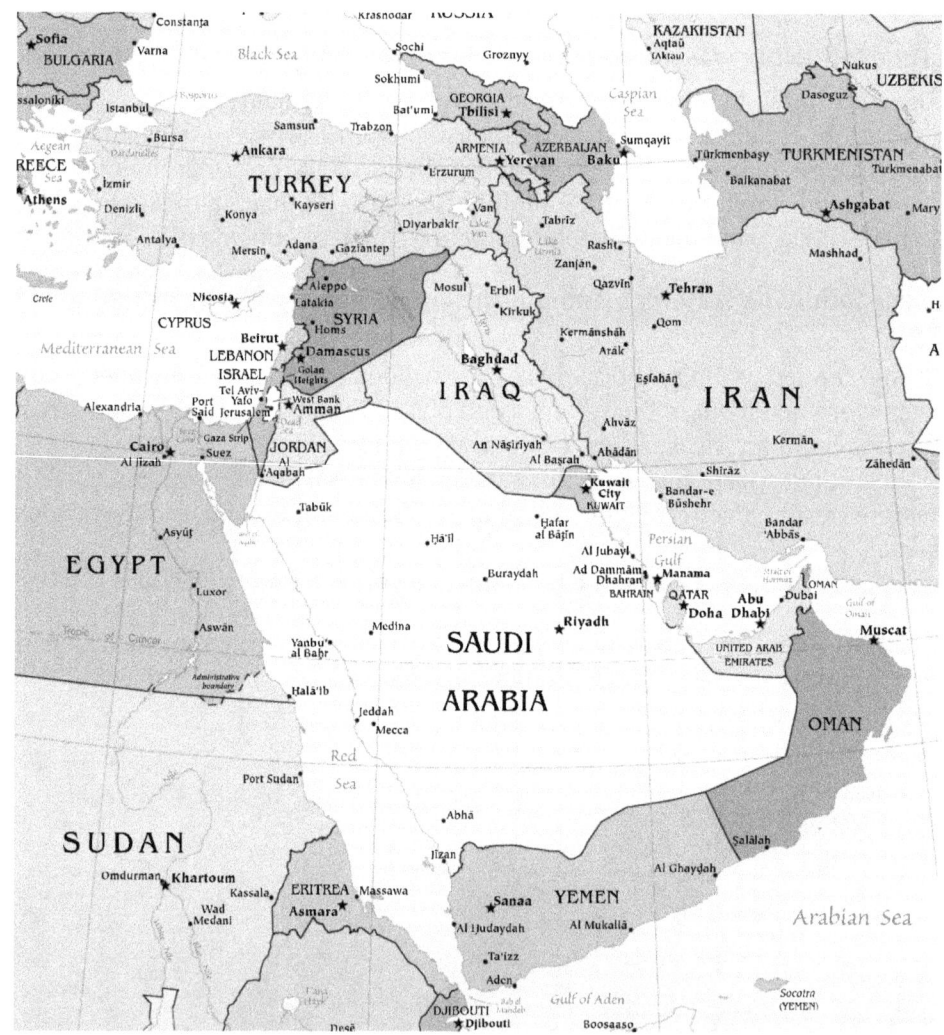

41. The map above depicts what area, specifically?
    a. The place of origin for all major world religions.
    b. The Holy Land
    c. The Middle East
    d. The Strait of Gibraltar

42. Which of the following is an incorrect statement about the Korean War?
    a. It began as a civil war, but eventually it turned into a proxy war
    b. The Democratic People's Republic of Korea obtained aid from China
    c. Only the United States supported the Republic of Korea
    d. The Democratic People's Republic of Korea obtained aid from USSR
    e. Both the UN and the USA supported the Republic of Korea

43. Which of the following is not true about the use of computers in America?
    a. Mainframe computers existed in America beginning in 1946.
    b. The invention of microprocessors in the 1970s enabled the creation of a PC.
    c. The PC allowed the widespread use of computers by private citizens.
    d. PCs enabled home computer use, but had less impact on businesses.
    e. The Internet's origin was the Department of Defense's Arpanet in the 1960s.

44. Which of the following statements does not describe the average European diet BEFORE the expansion of trade routes?
    a. Europeans ate for survival, not enjoyment.
    b. They had an abundance of preservatives such as salt that could make food last longer.
    c. Grain-based foods such as porridge and bread were staple meals.
    d. Spices were unavailable.
    e. Luxury items such as tea, sugar, and coffee had not yet been introduced.

45. Which of the following statements is not true of the rash of witch hunts that took place in the 14th through 16th centuries in Europe?
    a. The witch hunts used the Inquisition's techniques for rooting out heretics.
    b. Many hunts followed careful legal codes.
    c. Much of the evidence used was based on hearsay.
    d. Belief in magic and superstition was commonplace even among educated Europeans.
    e. It is estimated that between 40,000 and 100,000 suspected witches were killed during the Early Modern period.

46. Which is an *incorrect* answer regarding the Luddites?
    a. This group constituted a British social movement.
    b. This group was made of artisanal weavers.
    c. This group was opposed to new textile machines.
    d. This group was famous for destroying machines.
    e. This group's name is now used for skilled artists.

47. Which of the following words are associated with commerce in the German states in the mid-19th century?
    a. Zollverein
    b. Realpolitik
    c. Schleswig
    d. Holstein
    e. Reichstag

48. Which of the following regarding AIDS during the 1980s is not correct?
    a. Cases of this new syndrome were first discovered in 1984.
    b. The infection causing AIDS spread quickly in intravenous drug users.
    c. Initially, AIDS spread quickly among male homosexuals.
    d. Cases of AIDS multiplied at an average of more than 8,000 each year.
    e. More than half of the reported cases of AIDS ended in death by 1988.

49. Who was not an early explorer of the Americas?
    a. Amerigo Vespucci.
    b. Ferdinand Magellan.
    c. John Cabot.
    d. Henry Hudson.
    e. Ignatius Loyola.

50. When Americans captured Fort Ticonderoga on Lake Champlain, who led them?
    a. Ethan Allen
    b. Benedict Arnold
    c. Richard Montgomery
    d. All of the above
    e. Ethan Allen and Benedict Arnold only

Refer to the following for question 51:

Current Commonwealth members (dark blue), former members (orange), and British Overseas Territories and Crown Dependencies (light blue)

In the Balfour Declaration of 1926, Britain and British Empire dominions agreed that they would now be "equal in status" and members of the British Commonwealth of Nations, with no member superior to the others.

51. What information can we learn from the map above?
  a. The Commonwealth has expanded since the Balfour Declaration.
  b. Britain maintains a colonial presence on every continent on earth.
  c. Few countries remain in the Commonwealth.
  d. The Commonwealth has lost members since it was originally established.
  e. Several countries are considering leaving the Commonwealth.

52. When was the first American transcontinental railroad finished?
  a. 1862
  b. 1890
  c. 1869
  d. 1865

53. Which of the following is considered to be the largest cause of death among Native Americans following the arrival of European colonists in North America?
  a. Wounds from wars with the European settlers
  b. Wounds from wars with the other Native American tribes
  c. European diseases
  d. Exposure during the wintry, forced marches on which the European settlers forced them

54. Which of the following statements is *not* true of the rash of witch hunts that took place in the 14th through 16th centuries in Europe?

   a. The witch hunts used the Inquisition's techniques for rooting out heretics.
   b. Many hunts followed careful legal codes.
   c. Much of the evidence used was based on hearsay.
   d. Belief in magic and superstition was commonplace even among educated Europeans.

55. In what modern-day country are the remains of the Mesopotamian civilization found?

   a. Afghanistan
   b. Iraq
   c. Türkiye
   d. Egypt
   e. Lebanon

Answer Key and Explanations for Test #3

1. C: The catalyst to the onset of World War I was the assassination of Austria's Archduke Franz Ferdinand by Serbian nationalists (C). The Austrians suspected the Serbian government of aiding these nationalists and made demands of Serbia that would bring that country under the control of Austria. When Serbian officials refused, Austria declared war on Serbia. While the Archduke's assassination was not done by Russians (B), Russia declared war on Austria in defense of Serbia. Being allied with Austria, Germany (D) then declared war on Russia in retaliation. Two days later, Germany also declared war on France, and France (E) declared war on Germany the next day, not only in response to Germany's declaration of war, but also to fulfill its promise to defend Belgium's neutrality since Germany had invaded Belgium the same day it declared war on Russia. All of these events started the First World War and also established the initial two opposing groups: the Allied powers, consisting of Russia, France, and Great Britain; and the Central Powers, consisting of Germany, Austria-Hungary, Bulgaria, and the Ottoman Empire.

2. A: Boris Yeltsin was a Russian politician who was instrumental in the breaking up of the USSR and the end of Communism in Russia. In 1991, he was elected President of the Russian Federation in Russia's first democratic election.

3. A: It is the BEST title for the list, The Causes of the 1935 Dust Bowl. The lack of ground cover was a cause of the Dust Bowl, but could also be considered a possible effect of dust storms also. But that is the only item on the list that would also be an effect of the Dust Bowl. The Sun Belt also had some years of drought, but the other items would not fit for Sun Belt as much, or for the Rust Belt except for possibly poor agricultural practices.

4. A: Mary is describing the effects of the War of 1812 through this graphic organizer, which she has done accurately in this graph. However, the boxes on the bottom are somewhat vague, describing independence from Britain and industrial growth. By re-organizing her graph, Mary will demonstrate that the Industrial Revolution grew out of the War of 1812. Because industrial production grew, a new railroad system was built, production and refining was increased, and America relied less on foreign imports. All of these boxes are effects, or supporting details, of the War of 1812 and the Industrial Revolution.

5. A: When the President sent federal troops, this caused the Whiskey Rebellion to end, which resolved the situation and added to the new government's credibility. It did not result in a setback for the government. It is true that the whiskey tax was central to Hamilton's revenue program (B). It is true that farmers in western states, including Pennsylvania, did not want to pay this tax (C). It is also true that in addition to objecting to the tax and refusing to pay it, a group of farmers in Pennsylvania terrorized tax collectors to make their point (D). It is true that Washington responded to the farmers' terrorism by sending around 15,000 soldiers to quell the Whiskey Rebellion (E) in 1794.

6. D: Oklahoma became the 46th state in America in 1907. The year 1900 (A) saw more than 30 Indian tribes relocated to what were the Indian Territories, while Texas ranchers began moving in, seeking new pasture. Settlers who crossed the borders ahead of government permission were called Sooners, which became the state nickname. In 1902 (B), Indian Territory tribal leaders attempted to form their own state, called Sequoyah. They held the Sequoyah Constitutional Convention in 1905 (C). They petitioned Congress with overwhelming residential support, but

Congress, wanting to join the Indian and Oklahoma Territories into one state, rejected the idea of separate statehood for each.

7. B: Paul of Tarsus played one of the most significant roles in the development of the early Christian Church.

8. E: All of these explorers were involved in the search for a Northwest Passage (i.e. a route over water from North America to Asia). Giovannia da Verrazzano (A) of Italy sailed under the French flag in 1524 and went up the coast of America from what is now North Carolina to what is now Maine. John Cabot (B) of Italy, also known as Giovanni Caboto, was commissioned by England to look for a Northwest Passage in 1497, and was the first European to come to North America since the Vikings claimed the land in England's name. Jacques Cartier (C) made three expeditions to America beginning in 1534 on behalf of France. He explored and claimed the St. Lawrence River area, progressing as far as Montreal in Canada. Ferdinand Magellan (D) of Portugal discovered a water route around the southern tip of South America in 1519. When he set sail five years after Verrazzano, Magellan hoped to follow in the earlier explorer's footsteps.

9. A: Knights Templar is the name by which the Poor Fellow-Soldiers of Christ and of the Temple of Solomon is more commonly called. The Knights Templar began as a small and impoverished order intended to serve as a fighting force in the Holy Land, but soon grew into a large organization and a favorite charity. As the Templars' resources grew, their operations did and their activities included the management of an early form of banking that permitted travelers to carry less money with them, making the travelers a less tempting target for thieves and increasing their safety.

10. C: Francis Bacon was an English philosopher who promoted the scientific method. Roger Bacon was a monk who argued in favor of scientific experimentation to better understand the physical world. Ambroise Paré is considered the father of modern surgery. Andreas Vesalius made an important impact on the study of anatomy.

11. B: The Black Death refers to the plague that swept through 14th century Europe. Bubonic plague, brought in by rats on shipping vessels, is believed to have been the primary cause, though some question this theory.

12. C: Postal services did not charge extra to deliver anti-slavery mail as a reaction to the abolitionist movement. Rather, the postal services in the South would not even deliver such mail. People in the South did adopt a defensive position against abolitionism, including quoting the Bible in an attempt to justify slavery (A). They also trotted out "scientific" arguments about the innate "inferiority" of African black people (B), as if this would somehow make it acceptable to enslave other people, even if it were true. Dissension was not allowed, and the South became extremely repressive of any discussion, increasing the closing off of the South (D) from the North and West. In this repressive atmosphere, free thinking and open-minded inquiry were impossible, so creative and scholarly written expression withered and became severely limited (E). Writers like Edgar Allan Poe and William Gilmore Simms were rare exceptions to the rule.

13. A: The League of Nations was an international organization formed to maintain peace and security in the post-World War I world. The fact that the United States did not join seriously weakened the League.

14. C: While there would have been some understanding of scurvy by 1604, its exact causes and cure would not have been widespread knowledge. Champlain did not identify the disease as scurvy, which the writer of the passage alludes to with the expression "a disease now believed to be scurvy." While scurvy and pellagra are both linked to vitamin deficiencies, Choice A is false, and there is no information in the passage to support it. Choice B is also unsupported by the passage and factually incorrect. Choice D is incorrect because knowledge of the disease in 1497 shows that there was some awareness of scurvy in 1604. While choice E is true, there was some understanding of the disease in Europe during Samuel de Champlain's time, and a lack of understanding of the cause of scurvy would not prohibit someone at the time from recognizing its symptoms.

15. C: If a determinant of demand increases, demand will increase. That means that the demand curve will shift to the right, causing an increase in both the equilibrium price and the equilibrium quantity. An increase in a determinant of demand will not cause any movement to the supply curve.

16. E: Sheepherding (E) was not one of the first industries to develop in the Western US; rather, sheepherding, along with farming, eventually supplanted the cattle industry. Initial developments in Western expansion included mining for gold (A) and silver (B), which could only be accomplished by large mining companies once individual prospectors had exhausted the shallow veins of ore. The 1878 Timber and Stone Act advanced the lumber industry (C) by allowing individuals to buy low-priced land, whereupon large companies funded these individuals and then transferred the individual land purchases to their corporations. With the large grasslands in the West, cattle (D) initially became a big industry as well as mining and lumber. However, cattlemen were soon deprived of grazing land by famers and sheepherders (E) who also settled the Great Plains.

17. D: The state that was not one of the original seven to secede from the Union and form the Confederacy was North Carolina. South Carolina (A) was the first state to secede from the Union on December 20, 1860. By February, 1861, the other six states to follow South Carolina in secession were Alabama, Georgia (B), Florida (E), Mississippi, Louisiana, and Texas (C). Virginia, Arkansas, North Carolina (D), and Tennessee all seceded from the Union and joined the Confederacy after April 15, 1861.

18. D: Embargo, sanction, and military intervention would be a sequence of actions which go from more to less peaceful on the continuum. The other items on the list, A, B, C, and E, do not follow this order.

19. B: Though Choices (C), (D), and (E) apply to Da Vinci, the question describes him as a man with great learning and skills in a variety of fields, which is the definition of a Renaissance Man.

20. B: The Pilgrims' initial intention had been to settle in Northern Virginia where England had already established a presence. As there was no government in place in New England, some Pilgrims believed that they had no legal or moral duty to remain with the Pilgrims' new colony which needed their labor and support. Because of this, the Mayflower Compact created a government in New England and was signed on board the Mayflower on November 11, 1620 by each of the adult men who made the journey. The Compact's life was relatively short, due to its being superseded by the Pierce Patent in 1621 which had been signed by the king of England and had granted the Pilgrims the right of self-government in Plymouth. In spite of its short lifespan, the Mayflower Compact is credited with being North America's first constitution.

21. A: Historians today would be least likely to agree that Western civilization has not been as influential as other civilizations (A). To the contrary, historians tend to believe that by 2000, the history of Western civilization makes it one of the most, or the most, influential civilization in the world. Historians do agree that communism originated in Western civilization (B), as did democracy (C). They also note that significant modern advances in technology, such as telephones, televisions, radios, automobiles, airplanes, and computers; and in education, in the form of Western universities, all took place in Western civilization (D). Historians would certainly agree that one example of the many radical changes that Western civilization has seen from 1648 to 2000 is that in 1648, there were no nations because the idea of a nation had not yet been conceived (E). Other great changes in this time period include the change from one basic view of the world that most people had in 1648, centered on God's power, to the extensive multiplicity of world views, beliefs, and ideas existing in the 2000s; the decrease in work hours and increase in leisure hours from 1648 to 2000; and the improvement in standards of living over this period of time.

22. C: Pennsylvania is most closely associated with William Penn, a Quaker of the Society of Friends. Penn hoped to establish a colony where Quakers would be free to practice their religion. This colony offered religious tolerance toward many other religions as well; Dutch Mennonites and German Baptists were among those who came to Pennsylvania. The desire for freedom of the press was not a salient concern in the motivation for colonizing Pennsylvania; this eliminates option A. Although some European colonists came to Pennsylvania for economic reasons, these are not best understood in terms of escaping high taxes or trade restrictions. This eliminates options B and D.

23. B: The *Dialogue Concerning the Two Chief World Systems* was written in 1632 by Galileo Galilei. Two characters debate the merits and flaws of the Ptolemaic model, the Earth was the center of the heavens, and the Copernican model, the Earth was not the center of the universe. The Inquisition forced Galileo to publicly retract his support for the Copernican model.

24. C: The US-Soviet race to the moon is an example of a circumstance where a chronological point of view would be appropriate as each nation's advances fueled the other nation's desire to surpass its Cold War rival.

25. C: It is not true that Congress rejected Clinton's health care proposal wholesale (C). Although his motion for universal coverage was denied by Congress, some parts of Clinton's proposal were passed into law, such as the Children's Health Insurance Program (CHIP).

Clinton announced in 1993 that he would suspend the ban on gays in the military. However, due to objections by antigay interests, Clinton changed his policy and reached an agreement with Congress such that military management could not question personnel regarding sexual orientation, and service persons could not offer any information on the subject—the "don't ask-don't tell" policy (A). In 1993, Clinton's administration passed the Family and Medical Leave Act, which required most companies with at least 50 employees to give employees up to 12 weeks of unpaid leave for family bonding and/or to care for an immediate family member who is ill. The act also requires employers to maintain health benefits during that leave. As the federal deficit continued to grow, Clinton made a financial plan that included raising taxes and lowering federal spending by cutting government jobs and other means. The plan was narrowly passed by Congress (D).

26. A: What is not true about the British Empire is (A): By the beginning of the 20th century, it controlled over 20% of the world's population, not 25%. (Over 20% is still a remarkable proportion.) It is true that the British Empire began the program of Rhodes Scholars and Scholarships (B), which still exists today. This program was named after its founder, Cecil Rhodes, an important person in England's imperial rule of South Africa who wanted certain African colonial students to get educations in England and then come home to help their fellow Africans learn to adopt British culture. The African country of Zimbabwe was also previously named Rhodesia after Cecil Rhodes (C). It is true that despite the impressive size of the British Empire's conquests between the 19th and 20th centuries, the actual landmass of the country of Great Britain is much smaller than the US state of California (D). Because (A) is not true, (E), all of these, is incorrect.

27. D: All the laws (D) named were instrumental in spurring westward migration to the Great Plains. The Homestead Act (A), passed in 1862, gave settlers 160 acres of land at no monetary cost in exchange for a commitment to cultivating the land for five years. The Timber Culture Act (B), passed in 1873, gave the settlers 160 acres more of land in exchange for planting trees on one quarter of the acreage. The Desert Land Act (C), passed in 1877, allowed buyers who would irrigate the land to buy 640 acres for only 25 cents an acre. Thus, (D), all of these laws were instrumental in spurring westward migration to the Great Plains during that period, is correct.

28. B: It is not true that the US and Germany were equal in leading industry (B). Although Germany's factories did more than quadruple in number (A) during the Second Industrial Revolution, evidencing enormous growth, the United States was still the world leader of industry. The oil and steel industries (C and D) were two of the most important contributors to additional industrial development. Though large corporations (such as the British East India Company) had previously existed, the Second Industrial Revolution beginning in the late 19th century was the time when "mega" corporations, as we are now familiar with them, came into being (E) all over the Western Hemisphere, but particularly in the United States, due in large part to the immigration of millions of Europeans (see question #71).

29. E: Machiavelli's book *The Prince* promoted a shrewd approach to politics, aimed at maintaining power. Petrarch was a humanist poet, famous for his sonnets. Castiglione wrote a novel disguised as fiction that revealed the lives of government officials and royalty. Brunelleschi was an architect famous for the Duomo. Botticelli was an influential painter from Florence, Italy.

30. B: Hernando de Soto led an expedition of 600 men to southeastern America between 1539 and 1541, getting as far west as Oklahoma and discovering the Mississippi River in the process. Francisco Vasquez de Coronado (A) and his men made an expedition to southwestern America between 1540 and 1542, traveling from Mexico across the Rio Grande and going to New Mexico, Arizona, Texas, Oklahoma, and Kansas. In the process, they became some of the first European explorers to see the Grand Canyon. Hernando Cortes (C) conquered the Aztecs of Mexico in 1519. Juan Ponce de Leon (D) explored Florida looking for the Fountain of Youth and for gold in 1513. At the time, he also claimed Florida for Spain. Panfilio de Narvaez (E) led an expedition to the Gulf Coast area of America in 1528. It failed, and only a few of the hundreds of men who participated in this expedition returned.

31. C: Following the Thirty Years' War, the Hapsburg Empire, ruled by the monarchy of the Hapsburg royal family, included many Muslims from Hungary after it was freed from the rule of the Turkish Ottoman Empire. It is not correct to say that the Hapsburg Empire was stable or homogenous like Prussia following the war (A). Unlike Prussia, the Hapsburg Empire was made up of a diverse population. This heterogeneity made the empire unstable for the majority of its existence until it ended after World War I. The diversity in the Hapsburg Empire caused major differences among its members in languages and cultures (D) and in religious and political beliefs (E). As a result, even the empire's military forces did not run smoothly (B) as they were made up of people from various regions with different backgrounds, customs, and attitudes.

32. A: Roman civilization developed on the Tiber River, but it is not considered one of the earliest civilizations. Major civilizations developed along the other rivers listed: Chinese civilization developed in the Yangtze and Huang River valleys; Mesopotamian civilization emerged between the Tigris and Euphrates; and Egyptian culture developed in the Nile River valley.

33. B: The Thirty Years' War (1618-1648) in Europe was known as a "war of religion." It was fought among Lutherans, Catholics, and Calvinists in central Europe. It was not called a "war of economy"

(A) and moreover was not fought over economic issues. It was not called a "war of power" (C), even though it was fought over issues of political power. Indeed, power was more important to this war than was religion, for which this war was named; however, since church and state were not yet separated at this time, religion and politics were so intertwined that political plotting and the ensuing warfare always involved religious issues as well. As with economy, commerce, (D), was not used to describe this war. Although the treaty ending this war did cement changes to religious practices that were begun by the Protestant Reformation, the war itself was never designated as a "war of reform" (E).

34. C: The charter to found Georgia was not granted in 1765. It was granted to General James Oglethorpe in 1732. In fact, by 1752, Oglethorpe's group felt that they had failed with this colony. The original purpose of the Georgia colony was indeed to create a buffer zone between South Carolina and Florida (A), which was a Spanish territory then. There were numerous wars being fought in the area between British and American troops and other imperialist countries. Oglethorpe was a British philanthropist, and he and his followers did found the Georgia colony (B). Oglethorpe and his group, as trustees who ran the colony for its first 21 years, laid down a great many rules in an effort to guide the colony's administration and development. This practice, however, meant that few people wanted to settle there. The few who did constantly complained about all of the rules (D). These settlers were made up of former British subjects who had lived in poverty in Britain (E) and migrated in the hopes of achieving greater success in the New World.

35. B: By using antiseptics, Muslim doctors prevented the infection that often led to loss of limbs or life among Europeans. The other responses are opinion or not supported by the paragraph. We have no way of comparing the bravery of Muslim people with those of other faiths when facing surgery, so Choice A can be eliminated. Likewise, Choice C is incorrect; there would not be sufficient rise in silk use for sutures to account for an expanded silk market. It is not clear that the Muslims were the only people to have translations of the works of Aristotle, nor does the passage suggest such.

36. E: All of these factors were parts of President Richard M. Nixon's policy of "Vietnamization" after he took office in 1969. He directed that the US would give South Vietnam financial support (A) to assume more responsibility for the war (B). In gradual steps, Nixon started pulling American troops out of Vietnam (C), simultaneously stepping up the US bombing of North Vietnam (D).

37. B: The harsh educational techniques were practiced in Sparta, not Athens. The remaining choices are all reflections of Athenian educational practice.

38. A: The Medici were a powerful, wealthy family, famous for their financial contributions to artists in Florence.

39. A: Farmers moved from rural America to the cities to escape debts and low crop prices; at the same time, many immigrants from southern and Eastern Europe arrived in American cities. The influx of immigrants coupled with overcrowded housing resulted in city slums. . Reformers, such as Jacob Riis, author of *How the Other Half Lives* (published in1890), exposed these living conditions and expressed the need for improved housing. However, housing (A) was the one area of those listed that saw the least improvement. More progress was made to improve American urban infrastructure, such as sewer systems (B), fire fighting (C), street lighting (D), water supply (E), and pavement of streets and sidewalks.

40. B: The popular mood in the country during these years was not negative, but quite positive. In fact, this period was often called the "Era of Good Feelings." The country did undergo very fast economic and social development (A). In was, in fact, so fast that there was a severe depression in 1819 as a result (C). However, this depression was temporary, and economic growth soon resumed. America, begun with an agricultural economy, was experiencing increasing industrialization (D) during this time, moving away from farming as the basis of its economy and toward urbanization and industry. At the same time, the country's rapid growth and prosperity stimulated the existing trend of westward expansion (E), speeding up and intensifying the movements of pioneers to the western parts of the continent.

41. C: The area depicted by the map includes many countries considered to make up the Middle Eastern part of the world, which lies between Europe and Asia. Choice A is true for some major world religions, such as Islam, Christianity, and Judaism, yet there are other religions that have originated in other parts of the world, such as Buddhism and African traditional religions.

42. C: The incorrect statement is that the Republic of Korea (South Korea) was supported only by the United States. Instead, it was supported by the United States and by the United Nations (e). This conflict began as a civil war between North and South Korea, but as the other countries became involved, it turned into a proxy war (a). A proxy war is sponsored by outside powers; in this case, the outside powers were those involved in the Cold War. The Democratic People's Republic of Korea (the Communist side in North Korea) was supported by both China (b) and the USSR (d).

43. D: It is not true that PCs had less impact on businesses than on home users. Businesses had been using mainframe computers since around 1946 (A), after World War II. This use became more frequent as companies found them advantageous to tracking and eventually processing, billing and payroll records. Mainframe computers were so large that they occupied entire rooms. When microprocessors were developed in the 1970s, it became possible to create a much smaller computer, the Personal Computer or PC (B). Due to its much smaller size and price, the PC enabled home computer use for the first time (C). Following the invention of the PC, the Arpanet (Advanced Research Projects Agency Network), a system developed in the 1960s by the Department of Defense and the first packet-switching network in the world, became the model for a similar public system, the Internet (E). The development of the PC, along with that of the Internet and the World Wide Web, had a profound impact on the ways that businesses operated, which is why (D) is incorrect.

44. B: Preservatives such as salt were only introduced to the European diet after trade routes opened and these goods could be brought to Europe.

45. B: The witch hunts reflect a time when belief in magic and superstition was widespread. Many historians view them as a reaction to the social and economic changes of the Early Modern period.

46. E: The name "Luddite" is now used as a generalization, but not regarding skilled artists. Rather, it is used to describe anybody who reacts negatively against any kind of new technology and/or is opposed to technical progress. (For example, when personal computers or cell phones first became popular, people might have called someone who hated and refused to use them a Luddite.) The Luddites were a social movement in Britain (A) composed of skilled artisans who used handlooms to weave cloth (B) and who were opposed to the new machine looms (C). These machines could be run by low-paid, unskilled workers, so Luddites feared they would lose their higher-paying, skilled jobs as more manufacturers converted to machines, whereby they could produce far more fabric in a shorter time and also pay lower wages to more employees. The Luddites were known for sabotage such as breaking mechanized looms (D) and destroying wool and cotton mills. (Note: The name Luddite is derived from the name Ned Lud, or Ned Ludd, a man who may or may not have existed in the village of Anstey, Leicestershire. According to legend, he destroyed some stocking knitting frames around 1779. Once stories of this alleged event had spread, it became a popular English joke whenever such equipment was sabotaged to say, "Ned Ludd did it." This joke reflects the fact that machine saboteurs were usually of necessity anonymous. The Luddite movement began in 1811-1812 and took its name from this possibly imaginary hero.)

47. A: Of the German words listed, Zollverein (A) had to do with commerce in the German states in the mid-19th century. It was the name of the system of free trade used among the German states, which was facilitated by the railroads. Realpolitik (B) was Otto von Bismarck's term for politics based on reality and pragmatism, rather than on ideals or theoretical concepts. Bismarck believed in doing what was realistically possible rather than trying to achieve impossible goals. Schleswig (C) and Holstein (D) were the names of two northern territories, populated partly by Germans, which had been annexed by Denmark until Bismarck attacked and defeated Denmark, giving Schleswig to Prussia and Holstein to Austria; then Bismarck also secured Holstein from Austria in the Seven Weeks' War of 1866. Reichstag (E) is the German word for "Parliament," which was created for the North German Confederation, although it had little control compared to Bismarck and Kaiser Wilhelm.

48. A: AIDS Cases were not first discovered beginning in 1984, but were found beginning in 1981. The HIV (Human Immunodeficiency Virus) infection that leads to AIDS (Acquired Immune Deficiency Syndrome) spread quickly in users of intravenous drugs (B) as a result of sharing injection needles. Initially, it was also transmitted quickly among male homosexuals (C). It is true that cases of AIDS multiplied in excess of 8,000 times annually (D). By 1988, more than half of the reported cases of AIDS had resulted in deaths (E).

49. E: Ignatius Loyola founded an order of priests called the Society of Jesus, or Jesuits. Amerigo Vespucci was immortalized when German mapmakers named the new world after him. Magellan was a Portuguese explorer who led the first expedition to travel around the world. John Cabot claimed Newfoundland, Nova Scotia, and areas of New England for England. Henry Hudson explored much of what is now the northeastern United States.

50. E: Ethan Allen (A) and Benedict Arnold (B) led the troops that captured Fort Ticonderoga in May of 1775. Following this victory, on December 31 of 1775, General Richard Montgomery (C) led an expedition to Montreal and Quebec to try to enlist the aid of Canada in America's resistance to Britain. This expedition met with another expedition led by Benedict Arnold. Their assault on Quebec was not successful. Montgomery was killed and Arnold was wounded. Since answer (E) is correct, answer (D) All of the above is incorrect.

51. D: As the map shows, both Ireland and Zimbabwe are former members of the Commonwealth, so the Commonwealth has lost some membership. Choice A is partly true, as newly independent former British colonies became members of the Commonwealth (increasing the total number of members), but this did not result in an overall geographical expansion of the Commonwealth. Choice B might appear to be true, but Commonwealth members are not colonies of the United Kingdom. Also, there are no British colonies or Commonwealth members in Antarctica. Choice C is false, as the map reveals. As for choice E, this has been true throughout much of the Commonwealth's history, but this is not depicted on the map.

52. C: The first transcontinental railroad was finished in 1869 (C) on May 10. Construction on the railroad was begun in 1862 (A) but not completed until seven years later. After completion, economic depression prevented more railroad building until the 1890s (B). In 1865 (D), there were 35 000 miles of railroad track in the country; by 1890 (B), there were 200 000 miles. The first transcontinental railroad connected the Central Pacific Railroad, which began in Sacramento, California, to the Union Pacific Railroad, which began in Omaha, Nebraska, in Utah.

53. C: While wounds from war most certainly killed more than a few, European disease laid waste to vast swaths of Native American people who had no immunity to the foreign diseases which the Europeans carried. The forced marches took place in the mid-19th century under Andrew Jackson's presidency and are thus removed from the time frame in question.

54. B: The witch hunts reflect a time when belief in magic and superstition was widespread. Many historians view them as a reaction to the social and economic changes of the Early Modern period.

55. B: The Mesopotamian civilization developed in the Tigris and Euphrates River Valley, an area now controlled by Iraq. None of the other answers encompass this region.

How to Overcome Test Anxiety

Just the thought of taking a test is enough to make most people a little nervous. A test is an important event that can have a long-term impact on your future, so it's important to take it seriously and it's natural to feel anxious about performing well. But just because anxiety is normal, that doesn't mean that it's helpful in test taking, or that you should simply accept it as part of your life. Anxiety can have a variety of effects. These effects can be mild, like making you feel slightly nervous, or severe, like blocking your ability to focus or remember even a simple detail.

If you experience test anxiety—whether severe or mild—it's important to know how to beat it. To discover this, first you need to understand what causes test anxiety.

Causes of Test Anxiety

While we often think of anxiety as an uncontrollable emotional state, it can actually be caused by simple, practical things. One of the most common causes of test anxiety is that a person does not feel adequately prepared for their test. This feeling can be the result of many different issues such as poor study habits or lack of organization, but the most common culprit is time management. Starting to study too late, failing to organize your study time to cover all of the material, or being distracted while you study will mean that you're not well prepared for the test. This may lead to cramming the night before, which will cause you to be physically and mentally exhausted for the test. Poor time management also contributes to feelings of stress, fear, and hopelessness as you realize you are not well prepared but don't know what to do about it.

Other times, test anxiety is not related to your preparation for the test but comes from unresolved fear. This may be a past failure on a test, or poor performance on tests in general. It may come from comparing yourself to others who seem to be performing better or from the stress of living up to expectations. Anxiety may be driven by fears of the future—how failure on this test would affect your educational and career goals. These fears are often completely irrational, but they can still negatively impact your test performance.

Elements of Test Anxiety

As mentioned earlier, test anxiety is considered to be an emotional state, but it has physical and mental components as well. Sometimes you may not even realize that you are suffering from test anxiety until you notice the physical symptoms. These can include trembling hands, rapid heartbeat, sweating, nausea, and tense muscles. Extreme anxiety may lead to fainting or vomiting. Obviously, any of these symptoms can have a negative impact on testing. It is important to recognize them as soon as they begin to occur so that you can address the problem before it damages your performance.

The mental components of test anxiety include trouble focusing and inability to remember learned information. During a test, your mind is on high alert, which can help you recall information and stay focused for an extended period of time. However, anxiety interferes with your mind's natural processes, causing you to blank out, even on the questions you know well. The strain of testing during anxiety makes it difficult to stay focused, especially on a test that may take several hours. Extreme anxiety can take a huge mental toll, making it difficult not only to recall test information but even to understand the test questions or pull your thoughts together.

Effects of Test Anxiety

Test anxiety is like a disease—if left untreated, it will get progressively worse. Anxiety leads to poor performance, and this reinforces the feelings of fear and failure, which in turn lead to poor performances on subsequent tests. It can grow from a mild nervousness to a crippling condition. If allowed to progress, test anxiety can have a big impact on your schooling, and consequently on your future.

Test anxiety can spread to other parts of your life. Anxiety on tests can become anxiety in any stressful situation, and blanking on a test can turn into panicking in a job situation. But fortunately, you don't have to let anxiety rule your testing and determine your grades. There are a number of relatively simple steps you can take to move past anxiety and function normally on a test and in the rest of life.

Physical Steps for Beating Test Anxiety

While test anxiety is a serious problem, the good news is that it can be overcome. It doesn't have to control your ability to think and remember information. While it may take time, you can begin taking steps today to beat anxiety.

Just as your first hint that you may be struggling with anxiety comes from the physical symptoms, the first step to treating it is also physical. Rest is crucial for having a clear, strong mind. If you are tired, it is much easier to give in to anxiety. But if you establish good sleep habits, your body and mind will be ready to perform optimally, without the strain of exhaustion. Additionally, sleeping well helps you to retain information better, so you're more likely to recall the answers when you see the test questions.

Getting good sleep means more than going to bed on time. It's important to allow your brain time to relax. Take study breaks from time to time so it doesn't get overworked, and don't study right before bed. Take time to rest your mind before trying to rest your body, or you may find it difficult to fall asleep.

Along with sleep, other aspects of physical health are important in preparing for a test. Good nutrition is vital for good brain function. Sugary foods and drinks may give a burst of energy but this burst is followed by a crash, both physically and emotionally. Instead, fuel your body with protein and vitamin-rich foods.

Also, drink plenty of water. Dehydration can lead to headaches and exhaustion, especially if your brain is already under stress from the rigors of the test. Particularly if your test is a long one, drink water during the breaks. And if possible, take an energy-boosting snack to eat between sections.

Along with sleep and diet, a third important part of physical health is exercise. Maintaining a steady workout schedule is helpful, but even taking 5-minute study breaks to walk can help get your blood pumping faster and clear your head. Exercise also releases endorphins, which contribute to a positive feeling and can help combat test anxiety.

When you nurture your physical health, you are also contributing to your mental health. If your body is healthy, your mind is much more likely to be healthy as well. So take time to rest, nourish your body with healthy food and water, and get moving as much as possible. Taking these physical steps will make you stronger and more able to take the mental steps necessary to overcome test anxiety.

Mental Steps for Beating Test Anxiety

Working on the mental side of test anxiety can be more challenging, but as with the physical side, there are clear steps you can take to overcome it. As mentioned earlier, test anxiety often stems from lack of preparation, so the obvious solution is to prepare for the test. Effective studying may be the most important weapon you have for beating test anxiety, but you can and should employ several other mental tools to combat fear.

First, boost your confidence by reminding yourself of past success—tests or projects that you aced. If you're putting as much effort into preparing for this test as you did for those, there's no reason you should expect to fail here. Work hard to prepare; then trust your preparation.

Second, surround yourself with encouraging people. It can be helpful to find a study group, but be sure that the people you're around will encourage a positive attitude. If you spend time with others who are anxious or cynical, this will only contribute to your own anxiety. Look for others who are motivated to study hard from a desire to succeed, not from a fear of failure.

Third, reward yourself. A test is physically and mentally tiring, even without anxiety, and it can be helpful to have something to look forward to. Plan an activity following the test, regardless of the outcome, such as going to a movie or getting ice cream.

When you are taking the test, if you find yourself beginning to feel anxious, remind yourself that you know the material. Visualize successfully completing the test. Then take a few deep, relaxing breaths and return to it. Work through the questions carefully but with confidence, knowing that you are capable of succeeding.

Developing a healthy mental approach to test taking will also aid in other areas of life. Test anxiety affects more than just the actual test—it can be damaging to your mental health and even contribute to depression. It's important to beat test anxiety before it becomes a problem for more than testing.

Study Strategy

Being prepared for the test is necessary to combat anxiety, but what does being prepared look like? You may study for hours on end and still not feel prepared. What you need is a strategy for test prep. The next few pages outline our recommended steps to help you plan out and conquer the challenge of preparation.

STEP 1: SCOPE OUT THE TEST

Learn everything you can about the format (multiple choice, essay, etc.) and what will be on the test. Gather any study materials, course outlines, or sample exams that may be available. Not only will this help you to prepare, but knowing what to expect can help to alleviate test anxiety.

STEP 2: MAP OUT THE MATERIAL

Look through the textbook or study guide and make note of how many chapters or sections it has. Then divide these over the time you have. For example, if a book has 15 chapters and you have five days to study, you need to cover three chapters each day. Even better, if you have the time, leave an extra day at the end for overall review after you have gone through the material in depth.

If time is limited, you may need to prioritize the material. Look through it and make note of which sections you think you already have a good grasp on, and which need review. While you are studying, skim quickly through the familiar sections and take more time on the challenging parts.

Write out your plan so you don't get lost as you go. Having a written plan also helps you feel more in control of the study, so anxiety is less likely to arise from feeling overwhelmed at the amount to cover.

STEP 3: GATHER YOUR TOOLS

Decide what study method works best for you. Do you prefer to highlight in the book as you study and then go back over the highlighted portions? Or do you type out notes of the important information? Or is it helpful to make flashcards that you can carry with you? Assemble the pens, index cards, highlighters, post-it notes, and any other materials you may need so you won't be distracted by getting up to find things while you study.

If you're having a hard time retaining the information or organizing your notes, experiment with different methods. For example, try color-coding by subject with colored pens, highlighters, or post-it notes. If you learn better by hearing, try recording yourself reading your notes so you can listen while in the car, working out, or simply sitting at your desk. Ask a friend to quiz you from your flashcards, or try teaching someone the material to solidify it in your mind.

STEP 4: CREATE YOUR ENVIRONMENT

It's important to avoid distractions while you study. This includes both the obvious distractions like visitors and the subtle distractions like an uncomfortable chair (or a too-comfortable couch that makes you want to fall asleep). Set up the best study environment possible: good lighting and a comfortable work area. If background music helps you focus, you may want to turn it on, but otherwise keep the room quiet. If you are using a computer to take notes, be sure you don't have any other windows open, especially applications like social media, games, or anything else that could distract you. Silence your phone and turn off notifications. Be sure to keep water close by so you stay hydrated while you study (but avoid unhealthy drinks and snacks).

Also, take into account the best time of day to study. Are you freshest first thing in the morning? Try to set aside some time then to work through the material. Is your mind clearer in the afternoon or evening? Schedule your study session then. Another method is to study at the same time of day that you will take the test, so that your brain gets used to working on the material at that time and will be ready to focus at test time.

STEP 5: STUDY!

Once you have done all the study preparation, it's time to settle into the actual studying. Sit down, take a few moments to settle your mind so you can focus, and begin to follow your study plan. Don't give in to distractions or let yourself procrastinate. This is your time to prepare so you'll be ready to fearlessly approach the test. Make the most of the time and stay focused.

Of course, you don't want to burn out. If you study too long you may find that you're not retaining the information very well. Take regular study breaks. For example, taking five minutes out of every hour to walk briskly, breathing deeply and swinging your arms, can help your mind stay fresh.

As you get to the end of each chapter or section, it's a good idea to do a quick review. Remind yourself of what you learned and work on any difficult parts. When you feel that you've mastered the material, move on to the next part. At the end of your study session, briefly skim through your notes again.

But while review is helpful, cramming last minute is NOT. If at all possible, work ahead so that you won't need to fit all your study into the last day. Cramming overloads your brain with more information than it can process and retain, and your tired mind may struggle to recall even previously learned information when it is overwhelmed with last-minute study. Also, the urgent nature of cramming and the stress placed on your brain contribute to anxiety. You'll be more likely to go to the test feeling unprepared and having trouble thinking clearly.

So don't cram, and don't stay up late before the test, even just to review your notes at a leisurely pace. Your brain needs rest more than it needs to go over the information again. In fact, plan to finish your studies by noon or early afternoon the day before the test. Give your brain the rest of the day to relax or focus on other things, and get a good night's sleep. Then you will be fresh for the test and better able to recall what you've studied.

STEP 6: TAKE A PRACTICE TEST

Many courses offer sample tests, either online or in the study materials. This is an excellent resource to check whether you have mastered the material, as well as to prepare for the test format and environment.

Check the test format ahead of time: the number of questions, the type (multiple choice, free response, etc.), and the time limit. Then create a plan for working through them. For example, if you have 30 minutes to take a 60-question test, your limit is 30 seconds per question. Spend less time on the questions you know well so that you can take more time on the difficult ones.

If you have time to take several practice tests, take the first one open book, with no time limit. Work through the questions at your own pace and make sure you fully understand them. Gradually work up to taking a test under test conditions: sit at a desk with all study materials put away and set a timer. Pace yourself to make sure you finish the test with time to spare and go back to check your answers if you have time.

After each test, check your answers. On the questions you missed, be sure you understand why you missed them. Did you misread the question (tests can use tricky wording)? Did you forget the information? Or was it something you hadn't learned? Go back and study any shaky areas that the practice tests reveal.

Taking these tests not only helps with your grade, but also aids in combating test anxiety. If you're already used to the test conditions, you're less likely to worry about it, and working through tests until you're scoring well gives you a confidence boost. Go through the practice tests until you feel comfortable, and then you can go into the test knowing that you're ready for it.

Test Tips

On test day, you should be confident, knowing that you've prepared well and are ready to answer the questions. But aside from preparation, there are several test day strategies you can employ to maximize your performance.

First, as stated before, get a good night's sleep the night before the test (and for several nights before that, if possible). Go into the test with a fresh, alert mind rather than staying up late to study.

Try not to change too much about your normal routine on the day of the test. It's important to eat a nutritious breakfast, but if you normally don't eat breakfast at all, consider eating just a protein bar. If you're a coffee drinker, go ahead and have your normal coffee. Just make sure you time it so that the caffeine doesn't wear off right in the middle of your test. Avoid sugary beverages, and drink enough water to stay hydrated but not so much that you need a restroom break 10 minutes into the test. If your test isn't first thing in the morning, consider going for a walk or doing a light workout before the test to get your blood flowing.

Allow yourself enough time to get ready, and leave for the test with plenty of time to spare so you won't have the anxiety of scrambling to arrive in time. Another reason to be early is to select a good seat. It's helpful to sit away from doors and windows, which can be distracting. Find a good seat, get out your supplies, and settle your mind before the test begins.

When the test begins, start by going over the instructions carefully, even if you already know what to expect. Make sure you avoid any careless mistakes by following the directions.

Then begin working through the questions, pacing yourself as you've practiced. If you're not sure on an answer, don't spend too much time on it, and don't let it shake your confidence. Either skip it and come back later, or eliminate as many wrong answers as possible and guess among the remaining ones. Don't dwell on these questions as you continue—put them out of your mind and focus on what lies ahead.

Be sure to read all of the answer choices, even if you're sure the first one is the right answer. Sometimes you'll find a better one if you keep reading. But don't second-guess yourself if you do immediately know the answer. Your gut instinct is usually right. Don't let test anxiety rob you of the information you know.

If you have time at the end of the test (and if the test format allows), go back and review your answers. Be cautious about changing any, since your first instinct tends to be correct, but make sure you didn't misread any of the questions or accidentally mark the wrong answer choice. Look over any you skipped and make an educated guess.

At the end, leave the test feeling confident. You've done your best, so don't waste time worrying about your performance or wishing you could change anything. Instead, celebrate the successful completion of this test. And finally, use this test to learn how to deal with anxiety even better next time.

> **Review Video: Test Anxiety**
> Visit mometrix.com/academy and enter code: 100340

Important Qualification

Not all anxiety is created equal. If your test anxiety is causing major issues in your life beyond the classroom or testing center, or if you are experiencing troubling physical symptoms related to your anxiety, it may be a sign of a serious physiological or psychological condition. If this sounds like your situation, we strongly encourage you to seek professional help.

Online Resources

Due to our efforts to try to keep this book to a manageable length, we've created a link that will give you access to all of your online resources:

mometrix.com/resources719/apworldhistory-27797

www.ingramcontent.com/pod-product-compliance
Lightning Source LLC
Chambersburg PA
CBHW060255240426
43673CB00047B/1930